# THE FIRST COMMISSION

Be Fruitful
Multiply
Fill the Earth
Subdue It
Reign

## DON ATKIN

*Cover Design by Denise Douglas*

# DEDICATION

A specific dedication of one of my books to my bride of nearly sixty years is long overdue.

She has helped to get all of my books proofed and edited, written one book of her own and co-authored one with me. Moreover, Barbara has been used of God—first, to bring me to Christ,[1] then to bring me to maturity. (I was my wife's first child!)

The substance of this book has been worked out and proven in the laboratory of our marriage, home and lifetime together. It would be easy to flippantly say, "Works for us!" But, we have the memories of the process to buffet us.

Barbara has always seen herself as my helpmate, and has done it well. She was and remains an exemplary mother and homemaker. *Her children rise up and call her blessed.*[2] She is profoundly loved and honored by our twelve grandchildren. And those of the sixteen great-grandchildren who are old enough, run to her for hugs.

One of my highest priorities is to "wash" her in every way that helps her to be all that she is meant to be in Christ. She has not been "*just* a housewife, mother and homemaker." Undoubtedly, getting a job would have been the easier road. She has discipled many young women, including our daughters, into the fullness of their womanhood. She has been and remains a courageous woman of faith whose example *excels them all.*

> *Who can find a virtuous wife?*
> *For her worth is far above rubies.*
> *The heart of her husband safely trusts her.*[3]

---

[1] 1 Peter 3:1-6
[2] Proverbs 31:28
[3] Proverbs 31:10-11

# "FEEDBACK"

# CONTENTS

# Foreword

# TI IE GLORY OF GOD IN MOSES' FACE

*God said to Moses: "Now write down these words, for by these words I've made a covenant with you and Israel."*

*Moses was there with God forty days and forty nights. He didn't eat any food; he didn't drink any water. And he wrote on the tablets the words of the covenant, the Ten Words.*

*When Moses came down from Mount Sinai carrying the two Tablets of The Testimony, he didn't know that the skin of his face glowed because he had been speaking with God. Aaron and all the Israelites saw Moses, saw his radiant face, and held back, afraid to get close to him.* [1]

Moses was 80 years old at the time of the Exodus, and at Sinai when the "Ten Commandments" were given. Whatever happened to Moses during those forty days and forty nights spent with God left him with not only the glory of God in his face, but also the revelation of God in his heart!

Surely, God helped him to write Genesis, Exodus, Leviticus, Numbers and Deuteronomy. What an astounding accomplishment! Surely, the Holy Spirit inspired him to record in such detail the heart of God in legal terms, yet with compelling drama that could be understood by men of flesh.

More than candlelight illuminated his penmanship enabling Moses to leave behind such a magnificent contribution to generations from the patriarchs and prophets to Messiah, and on to those who are Messiah's disciples. His heaven-sent words are now bound in our hearts to be discovered in the unfolding dramas of our lives.

---

[1] Exodus 34:27-30 TM

The Creation Story encompasses so much yet to be unearthed and applied. First in canonical order, Genesis is a work of art by a skilled wordsmith who obviously had heaven's breath guiding his thoughts and his hand.

God's Commission to Adam and Eve was basically lost from sight when they settled for inferior fruit, and has not yet been fully recovered. Yet, there it is, recorded by Moses for our inspiration and obedience.

*The First Commission*[2] remains for eternity a few simple words that are to both constrain and guide our entire lives. I cannot help but to be overwhelmed with this evidence of a profound download allotted to Moses during those days and nights on Sinai.

> *Male and Female He created them.  Then God blessed them.*

Thus the mystery of life itself began to unfold on the sixth day.

---

[2] Genesis 1:28

# Introduction
# <u>JESUS' GLORIOUS CHURCH</u>
## IN EVERY LOCALITY ON EARTH
### David Drew

*That He might present her to Himself a glorious church, not having spot or wrinkle or any such thing, but that she should be holy and without blemish.*[1]

God is perfect in oneness. And His intention is (and always has been) that His people be the same. Just like the people in Jeremiah's day, we have changed our glory for one that has NO power to bring change and transformation. Listen to what God said in Jeremiah's day and see if you agree that it is pertinent for today.

> *"But My people have changed their Glory for that which does not profit... for My people have committed two evils: they have forsaken Me, the fountain of living waters, and hewn for themselves cisterns - broken cisterns that can hold no water."*[2]

What a shocking thing it is when God's people in any generation, operate from a different "spirit," relying on their own initiatives, ideas, training, education, motivation, eloquence, charisma, natural gifts, culture of the day, and the traditions of men, to carry out God's work.

> *"And you shall know the truth, and the truth shall make you free."*[3]

*Truth* is the only thing that never changes and cannot fail. It stands forever because **Jesus** is the source of all truth. He is the way, **Truth** and the life. He is the Alpha and the Omega, the first and last, the beginning and the end, and, He existed before all things.

---

[1] Ephesians 5:27
[2] Jeremiah 2:11-13
[3] John 8:32

The *truth* is that **Jesus** is the appointed Heir of all things. He created the worlds and the outer reaches of space. He made, produced, operated and arranged them in order.

The *truth* is that He is the sole expression of the glory of God. He is the perfect example and the very image of God, upholding, maintaining, and guiding the universe by the word of His power.[4]

And the *truth* is that He is the first-born Son, and you and I are given the opportunity to be 'born-again' making us a members of the Body of Christ, and transforming us into "God class" beings. Now that's the *truth!*

We must face the fact however, that there is an ever-increasing *darkness* covering the earth as a result of the absence of truth. Truth brings light and life. Deception and ignorance bring darkness and death.

The vast majority of Christian people are motivated to promote *their* church, *their* ministry, *their* program, *their* pastor, *their* music ministry... all in order to make a *"name for themselves"* just like those who built the Tower of Babel.[5] By so doing, we Christians, are also walking in darkness, and not allowing The Light to shine. **Jesus** is NOT the central focus.

The greatest threat for humanity in the 21st century is not terrorist groups, or the threat of nuclear war, or global warming, or the increasing number of world leaders who want to eliminate all reference of there being a God above, or false religions.

The greatest threat to humanity is a self-satisfied, "rich," sectarian Church that is competitive, and determined to remain independent from most other Christians! This Church system bears NO resemblance to the Church that Jesus said He would build, *"and the gates of Hades shall not prevail against it."*[6] Nor does it bear any resemblance to the Church Jesus prayed to Father for in John

---

[4] Read Hebrews 1 in the Amplified Bible
[5] Genesis 11:4
[6] Matthew 16:18

17:21-23 that is destined to be perfectly one just as Jesus and Father!

The ever-increasing darkness pervading the earth is being exacerbated by a man-centered Church, who, in its present state, has NO ability to stop the darkness. Unable, despite countless seminars, conferences and prayer initiatives, and millions of sermons preached to forgetful people. It is all useless if we are not prepared to repent and change our ways by becoming one church, one body, with Jesus as our Head.

Since Adam and Eve fell, it has been man's[7] default tendency to easily be led into Satan's schemes and ways. Satan's biggest fear and paranoia is that God's people would discover who they really are. He is terrified we would become TRUE sons of God just like Jesus, our Lord and King.

Using deceit and flattery, and working on man's innate need for identity, he has taken good Christian people on a search for self-discovery, find your destiny, self-promoting, ego-building exercises. And in the process they have built a grotesque version of God's Church made up of 34,000-38,000[8] separate denominations and ministries. Each group having its own identity, separate names, logos, branding, doctrines and activities, and in so doing they have effectively cut themselves off from the unlimited source of life and power... Jesus!

As a result, the world is unable to believe that Jesus was sent from God,[9] and views the church as just another form of obsolete, irrelevant religion.

**Jesus** has increasingly been hidden and veiled by this multi-faceted, multi-headed "church." More and more emphasis has been

---

[7] This is the natural tendency even for Christians.

[8] An Internet search will show research groups who estimate that there are between 34,000 and 38,000 separate Christian denominations, groups and cults in the world.

[9] John 17: 21-23

placed on separate denominational/church/ministry names. And CEO-type "senior pastors" are truly entrepreneurs and "would be" celebrities.

Because of the competitive race to build mega churches men have decided it's important to put on a good show full of "sensation" tickling activities. Jesus has been shut out of His Church in order for us to be "politically correct," keeping up with the times, and preaching false hyper-grace, life-style messages.

**Jesus** is portrayed in Revelation *outside* His Church trying to get in. He has been knocking at the door of the Church for 2000 years. This verse was part of a message to the Laodicean church that was described as *"lukewarm and neither hot nor cold"* and they said, *"I am rich, have become wealthy and have need of nothing..."*

Doesn't this describe much of our 21st century Church?[10] Can you see the gravity of the situation, and can you see that it's sin?

How can we refer to ourselves as collectively "The Body of Christ?" "Is Christ divided?" Paul was horrified that the Corinthians were beginning to develop factions in his day.

Let me ask you the same question. "Is Christ divided?" Your answer should be "No!" Christ can never be divided. The Godhead is one, and to truly be Christ's Body we must be ONE with Him and each other also. How can it be any other way?

In this excellent book you'll discover a very different Church. I urge you to pray and ask the Lord for revelation as you read what Don Atkin is sharing here. This is a profound work but not complicated. Men, in their "wisdom," complicate things when often the truth is simple to those with seeking eyes and hearts.

**David Drew,** A servant and son of God in Australia
Email: David@JesusChurch.info
Website:/www.JesusChurch.info

---

[10] Revelation 3:16, 20

# Chapter 1

# EFFECTIVE MINISTERS
# OF THE HOLISTIC GOSPEL
# OF THE KINGDOM

I printed out the cover design for this book on 8 X 10 glossy photo paper, and framed it. I am so inspired by it, challenged, and somewhat intimidated. If the book can just do justice to the cover!

I realize that "you can't tell a book by its cover." It is also true that you might be *drawn* to a book by its cover. Each of us is a book being written, a story being told that is much greater and deeper than our outward appearance.

> The resurrection of Christ also inaugurated something much broader—*the re-creation of the universe.*

Raw beauty may draw a few; but may also distract others. Raw beauty fades like Moses' glory. May our outward appearance not be a distraction from the glory of God we carry in our bosom. May we be so transparent that the Light of heaven and earth might reveal Him, not us.

> *Do not let your adornment be merely outward—arranging the hair, wearing gold, or putting on fine apparel—rather let it be the hidden person of the heart, with the incorruptible beauty of a gentle and quiet spirit, which is very precious in the sight of God.*[1]

"Life of the party" was my *reputation*. I had a reputation, but I did not have a *testimony*. *Reputations* are most often the result of our

---

[1] 1 Peter 3:3-4

own efforts, outward appearances, personalities, etc. *Testimonies* result from the *relationship* between the hidden person of the heart and the abiding Bridegroom.

I became a new creation in 1963, and was sent forth in 1968 with the witness of the local fellowship and the laying on of hands by the elders. I've been a zealot for the impossible. Refinement has redefined me. I am now zealous for what is not only possible, but absolutely essential.

- *The First Commission*[2] is my vision

- *The Great Commission*[3] is my strategy.

We are not only challenged to reclaim our roles insofar as *The First Commission* is concerned. If we are to be effective ministers of the holistic gospel of the kingdom, we will also need to submit to an inward chiropractic adjustment of heart so that we can readily bow in faith to that enormous authority and dignity that fills every letter of every word that is written—and do it together.

Jesus added the Great commission to *The First Commission* in preparation for the outpouring of the Holy Spirit upon all flesh.

We have been entrusted with two seeds—the natural seed and the spiritual *Seed*[4] Who enables us to fulfill the Great Commission. The seed of Adam had the life of God in it for reproduction and multiplication. That was what died when Adam sinned. Only the natural seed remained in His loins.

Today, we can be fruitful and multiply by virtue of the natural seed with the hope that each one in our progeny will become disciples of Christ. And, we can also be fruitful and multiply by virtue of the spiritual Seed, thereby bringing forth spiritual children. Do

---

[2] Genesis 1:28
[3] Matthew 28:19-20
[4] Galatians 3:16

you realize that you carry God's DNA and the Seed of Christ within your spirits?

It is the breath of God, the wind of the Spirit we need, blowing within and upon us as we ponder such a glorious possibility and embrace our parts in the unfolding drama surrounding those moments so long ago.

The resurrection makes it possible for the believer to be *a new creation*.[5] The resurrection of Christ also inaugurated something much broader—*the re-creation of the universe*. It is to that end that this book is aimed.

Pentecost was a second advent, Jesus coming in the Spirit to abide in His new creation body and to raise us into mature sonship. We would tend to give up before beginning, simply because of the magnitude of His purpose. Amazingly, God has not given up on us. He saw the end from the beginning, and wants to share His vision, its development and eventual fulfillment with His sons and daughters.

*Rediscovery* and *recovery* must fight their way through centuries of unbelief, religious denominations, and various cultural deteriorations. The emerging possibilities of realizing this "impossible dream" must find a home in our hearts.

> *The fundamental fact of existence is that this trust in God, this faith, is the firm foundation under everything that makes life worth living. It's our handle on what we can't see. The act of faith is what distinguishes our ancestors, set them above the crowd.*
>
> *By faith, we see the world called into existence by God's word, what we see created by what we don't see.[6]*

---

[5] 2 Cor 5:17
[6] Hebrews 11:1-3 TM

I wonder if *The Great Commission* spoken to His disciples just prior to His ascension was influenced by His acute awareness that they couldn't bear any more at that time. Just a few weeks earlier He had told them:

> *"I still have many things to say to you, but you cannot bear them now. However, when He, the Spirit of truth, has come, He will guide you into all truth; for He will not speak on His own authority, but whatever He hears He will speak; and He will tell you things to come. He will glorify Me, for He will take of what is Mine and declare it to you."*[7]

Is it not feasible that Jesus knew that *The First Commission* would be too much for them to grasp—especially prior to the coming of the Holy Spirit upon them? So He commissioned them to *disciple the nations,* which meant sharing everything that God had revealed to them. For them, this would be a "Great Commission." For them this would be HUGE!

They had no way of knowing that God would arrange for *devout men, from every nation under heaven*[8] to be brought to them! Nor did they realize that Father would send His Spirit upon all flesh, and make it possible for everyone to experience the fulfilling of Joel's prophecy,[9] AND hear the gospel of the kingdom in his own language![10]

If we would strategically devote ourselves to discipling others after the pattern of Jesus's earthly ministry, doing so in the Spirit who is leading us *into all truth,* would we not eventually be brought face-to-face with the truth about *The First Commission* and all of its implications?

---

[7] John 16:12-14
[8] Acts 2:5
[9] Joel 2:28-32
[10] Acts 2:8

# Chapter 2
# NEW WINE IS FOUND
# IN THE CLUSTER

*Thus says the Lord:*

*"As the new wine is found in the cluster, and one says, 'Do not destroy it, for a blessing is in it,' so will I do for My servants' sake, that I may not destroy them all."*[1]

Those who realize the *togetherness* implications of the kingdom of God can find hope in this promise of God.

*Purpose* is explored, discovered, developed and proven within our relationships with one another in Christ.

> **Purpose** is explored, discovered, developed and proven within our relationships with one another in Christ.

Jesus used the same metaphor as Isaiah when He identified Himself as: *"the true vine, and My Father is the vinedresser."*

- *Every branch in Me that does not bear fruit He takes away*

- *Every branch that bears fruit He prunes, that it may bear more fruit.*

- *By this My Father is glorified, that you bear much fruit; so you will be My disciples.*[2]

---

[1] Isaiah 65:8-9
[2] John 15:1-8

The kingdom was taken away from the nation (natural) Israel to be *given to a [holy] nation (chosen from all nations) that bears the fruits of it.*[3] To believe that we are disciples of Jesus simply on the basis of a statement of faith or church membership is tragically naïve. Father is looking for fruits!

Life begets life after kind. Kingdom fruit is the evidence of a *royal priesthood,* a *holy nation.* The assurance of fruit-bearing comes with abiding in Jesus. There is no way to do so apart from a living relationship birthed by the Holy Spirit.[4]

> *"Abide in Me, and I in you. As the branch cannot bear fruit of itself, unless it abides in the vine, neither can you, unless you abide in Me."*

We lived in the beautiful Napa Valley of California for two years, and then Sonoma County, California, some years later. Both are world-famous for quality wines. Gorgeous vineyards grace the landscape as far as one can see. I actually raised grapes years earlier. I know what it is to prune, tie, cultivate, fertilize and harvest the fruit of the vine.

Having lived now fifty years abiding in Jesus and allowing His life to make me a productive, fruitful branch, I still thrilled to be His disciple, a son of the kingdom, a joint heir with Christ, along with all my brothers and sisters.

If we took all of the clusters from a single branch, we could not produce much wine. Isaiah's prophetic insight speaks to our need to be clustered together with one another.

*The new wine is found in the cluster,* not in the culture—not in worldly cultures or in religious cultures.

Clustered together with one another in Christ is not only best for fruit-bearing, but is also the best protection from being assimilated

---

[3] Matthew 21:43
[4] John 3:1-8

by the prevailing worldly culture. We can rightly interact with and influence those around us from the safety of our "one-anothering" mutual accountability with other sons and daughters of the kingdom. We desperately need one another—all the more as we envision filling the earth with His glorious fruit.

> *Oh, Taste and see that the Lord is good; blessed is the man who trusts in Him!*[5]

We are to live life in communion with Jesus and one another. John put it this way:

> *We saw it, we heard it, and now we're telling you so you can experience it along with us, this experience of communion with the Father and His Son, Jesus Christ. Our motive for writing is simply this: We want you to enjoy this, too. Your joy will double our joy!*[6]

Let me be clear: While participating in the mysteries[7] in faith takes these practices well-beyond symbolism, the ultimate intention is having His life in us. Outward signs and symbols are to be manifestations of inward substances and realities.

> *We were buried with Him through baptism into death, that just as Christ was raised from the dead by the glory of the Father, even so we also should walk in newness of life.*[8]

> *"Whoever eats My flesh and drinks My blood has eternal life, and I will raise him up at the last day. For My flesh is food indeed, and My blood is drink indeed. He who eats My flesh and drinks My blood abides in Me, and I in him."*[9]

> *"Those who believe will lay their hands on the sick, and they will recover."*[10]

---

[5] Psalm 34:8

[6] 1 John 1:3-4 TM

[7] Baptism, the Eucharist, the Laying on of Hands, etc.

[8] Romans 6:4

[9] John 6:54-56

Each of these mysteries is beyond human reasoning, only to be experienced through faith. We are raised up with the newness of His life within us. We feast on Him daily, and His life within us brings healing to those around us, those upon whom we lay our hands.

While we do believe that our acts of obedience when done in faith bring a responsive fulfillment from our Father, our hope is not ultimately in sacrament or symbol (whatever our tradition). *Christ in us is the hope of glory!*[11]

We also can learn to look at one another with His eyes. Perhaps we can gain ground on that project by beginning to see ourselves through His eyes.

Jesus prepared us for a very important insight when He turned the water into wine:

> *There was a wedding in the village of Cana in Galilee. Jesus' mother was there. Jesus and His disciples were guests also. When they started running low on wine at the wedding banquet, Jesus' mother told Him, "They're just about out of wine."*
>
> *Jesus said, "Is that any of our business, Mother—yours or Mine? This isn't My time. Don't push Me."*
>
> *She went ahead anyway, telling the servants, "Whatever He tells you, do it."*
>
> *Six stoneware water pots were there, used by the Jews for ritual washings. Each held twenty to thirty gallons. Jesus ordered the servants, "Fill the pots with water." And they filled them to the brim.*

---

[10] Mark 16:18
[11] Colossians 1:27

26

*"Now fill your pitchers and take them to the hosts," Jesus said, and they did.*

*When the host tasted the water that had become wine (he didn't know what had just happened but the servants, of course, knew), he called out to the bridegroom, "Everybody I know begins with their finest wines and after the guests have had their fill brings in the cheap stuff. But you've saved the best till now!"*

*This act in Cana of Galilee was the first sign Jesus gave, the first glimpse of His glory. And His disciples believed in Him.*[12]

Jesus pleaded with His mother, and she quickly dismissed His appeal, He immediately submitted to and honored her. Her motherly ambition for her son was quite normal. She had treasured so much in her heart for thirty years. Jesus had been trained to *honor* His *father and mother*.

Here is a cautionary insight:

"Every time we see each other as *ordinary*, we turn the *wine* back into *water*."[13]

We are extraordinary because of the grace of God and the life of Christ within and upon us.

Smith Wigglesworth said, "I want to help you decide that, by the power of God, you will not be ordinary."

May our values help us to hold one another in the highest esteem! May His love for His creation constantly overwhelm us! Since we are to love our neighbor as ourselves, we should also hold ourselves in the highest esteem. We are extraordinary. I am extraordinary because of the grace of God.

---

[12] John 2:1-11 TM
[13] @Love Does

*If anyone is in Christ, he is a new creation; old things have passed away; behold, all things have become new![14]*

"The victorious Christian neither exalts nor downgrades himself. His interests have shifted from self to Christ. What he is, or is not, no longer concerns him. He believes that he has been crucified with Christ and he is not willing either to praise or deprecate such a man."[15]

We can safely accept and agree with God's evaluation of us—neither adding to nor taking away from the truth about who we are in Jesus. This is authentic humility.

Created and then subsequently redeemed for a place in Christ that no one else can fill, we should worship Him by our faithful obedience to Him.[16]

> *Beloved, we are [even here and] now God's children; it is not yet disclosed (made clear) what we shall be [hereafter], but we know that when He comes and is manifested, we shall [as God's children] resemble and be like Him, for we shall see Him just as He [really] is.*
>
> *And everyone who has this hope [resting] on Him cleanses (purifies) himself just as He is pure (chaste, undefiled, guiltless).[17]*

---

[14] 2 Corinthians 5:17
[15] A. W. Tozer
[16] John 14:21
[17] 1 John 3:2-3 AMP

28

# Chapter 3
# CANDOR, TRUTH AND LOVE

My father heart aches and weeps regularly over people in despair, the savagery, tragedy and terror in the world. I also grieve over the present condition of the church. I keep searching for clues, asking for direction on how to communicate in love the specifics that I have come to know—many of them through much tribulation.

> **Discipling the nations is the only strategy for fulfilling The *First Commission*.**

There is no conflict between truth and love. One of my heroes, named Paul, wrote these words as he coaxed and coached the church in Ephesus to move into *the unity of the faith* which comes with maturity:

> *Speaking the truth in love, (we) may grow up in all things into Him who is the head—Christ.*[1]

George Whitefield said, "Speak every time my dear brother as if it were your last."

Please choose to forgive me if I sound critical or judgmental. It is not my heart or the passion of Christ within me to be so misunderstood. What is written is necessarily confrontational.

"A boy in the streets, selling mince-pies, kept crying, 'Hot mince pies!' A person bought one of them, and found it quite cold. 'Boy,' said he, 'why do you call these pies hot?' 'That's the name they go by, sir,' said the boy. 'So there are plenty of people who are called Christians, but they are not Christians-that's the name they go by.'"[2]

---

[1] Ephesians 4:15

"Consciously or not Christians have accepted the ethos of our joyless and business-minded culture."[3]

Falling into the bottomless pit of today's shifting culture, mindlessly following the patterns of our forefathers, or blindly following after denominating traditions are not to be compared with a Spirit-infused life following Christ as His disciples.

> *For as many as are led by the Spirit of God, these are sons of God.*[4]

I want to address the church in the broadest of terms, realizing that *the wheat and tares* yet *grow together*. And, I do not want to risk uprooting the wheat by my premature efforts to gather out the tares.

> *"The kingdom of heaven is like a man who sowed good seed in his field; but while men slept, his enemy came and sowed tares among the wheat and went his way."*[5]

The church of the New Covenant had not yet been born when Jesus shared this parable. Today, there are many *tares* who believe that they are *wheat*! Yet, they do not abide in the vine nor do they yield abiding fruit![6]

Better to be awakened in time for repentance than to stand naked before God with no hope for salvation and reconciliation. Membership status in one of today's religious institutions is not to be misunderstood as the normal Christian life.

There is only one level of Christianity. There is no elite clergy sect. Neither is there a "plan B." We are either disciples of Jesus or we are not. *The disciples were first called Christians at Antioch.*[7] The terms *disciples* and *Christians* are synonymous.

---

[2] Charles Spurgeon
[3] A. Schmemann
[4] Romans 8:14
[5] Matthew 13:24-30
[6] John 15:6

30

They mean the same thing! You are not a Christian unless you are a disciple.[8]

Christian discipleship is costly:

- *If anyone comes to Me and does not hate his father and mother, wife and children, brothers and sisters, yes, and his own life, he cannot be My disciple.*

- *And whoever does not bear his cross and come after Me cannot be My disciple.*

- *So likewise, whoever of you does not forsake all that he has cannot be My disciple.*[9]

Jesus spoke the truth with candor and love.

This is not a venue issue! You will find loving brothers and sisters in every venue that you can imagine. Abiding in the vine and relationally interacting with other branches provides our hope for fruitfulness. *The new wine is found in the cluster.*

God made us, then whispered "Think symp*hony*, not *solo*."[10]

Each of us has a unique part to play. The orchestra is not complete without you; the body is not complete without you; the bride is not complete without you; and God's household is not complete without you!

It is not the physical architecture that makes the difference. We are talking about the condition of hearts and the knitting together of believers. The prophet Ezekiel was God's mouthpiece for this promise:

---

[7] Acts 11:26

[8] That commitment may be made in a moment—like right now at this moment.

[9] Luke 14:26-27, 33

[10] @Love Does

*"I will give you a new heart and put a new spirit within you; I will take the heart of stone out of your flesh and give you a heart of flesh.*

*"I will put My Spirit within you and cause you to walk in My statutes, and you will keep My judgments and do them. "Then you shall dwell in the land that I gave to your fathers; you shall be My people, and I will be your God.*

*"I will deliver you from all your uncleannesses. I will call for the grain and multiply it, and bring no famine upon you.*

*"And I will multiply the fruit of your trees and the increase of your fields, so that you need never again bear the reproach of famine among the nations. "*[11]

It is in our innermost being that we make connection with God and one another. We often use terms such as: "Jesus lives in my heart," realizing that He does not live in that organ that pumps the blood throughout our body. No, it's deeper than that. It is the spirit of man that connects with the Spirit of God, joined in complete oneness even as the Father and Son are one.[12]

The spiritual apparatus of heaven, borne in the person of Christ, connects with the spiritual apparatus in us prepared to receive Him, bow to Him, bring Him great pleasure, and glorify Him even as *the woman is the glory of man.*[13]

From within that innermost place, our faculties resonate one with another so that our wills turned toward God and yielded to the Holy Spirit allow His access, opening the door as He knocks, and He comes to sup with us, and then stays to *abide in us.*

He says, *"Come unto Me, all you who labor and are heavy laden, and I will give you rest. "*

---

[11] Ezekiel 36:26-30
[12] John 17:20-23
[13] 1 Corinthians 11:7

He says, *"Take My yoke upon you and learn from Me, for I am gentle and lowly in heart, and you will find rest for your souls."*

He says, *"For My yoke is easy and My burden is light."*[14]

He says, *"Come on! Put your head in the yoke!"*

What does Ephesians 4:20-24 have to say to us?

*"But you have not so learned Christ;"* (He didn't say, "You have not so learned *about* Christ.") We are not talking about learning *about* Him! We are talking about *learning Him*! Can you see the subtle difference? The deceiver's way would have you learning *about* a person that you are to *learn*!

Historians know a lot about George Washington and Abraham Lincoln. But they do not personally know them. Many religious folks know a lot about Jesus, but do not *know* Him.

*"If indeed you have heard Him and have been taught by Him as the truth is in Jesus."* The deceiver's translation: "If indeed you have heard about Him and have been taught about Him."

We can learn about dead people—George Washington, Robert E. Lee. History is cool. But life is LIFE! We need to *relate, know* and *learn* Jesus who is alive and well in the hearts of His disciples!

The *truth* is in Jesus. The fruit of His Spirit is *love*.

Writing to disciples of Jesus Christ, John stated:

> *You have an anointing from the Holy One, and you know all things.*[15]

*Christ in you, the hope of glory,*[16] is the total embodiment of all truth and love—abiding in His beloved disciples.

---

[14] Matthew 11:28-30
[15] 1 John 2:20
[16] Colossians 1:27

Imagine a library with high ceilings and shelves from floor to ceiling. It is larger than the largest library you have ever seen. It is the storehouse of all knowledge, nothing excepted. Jesus is that library, and He abides in His disciples.

There is nothing to be added—but a lifetime of discovery.

Not every volume is positive and upbeat. No. None of our lives are free from challenges. That would not be reality. Celebrating Jesus includes enjoying His counsel and enabling when faced with situations—making the right choices at the forks in the road inevitably give us.

"Lord, make me a crisis man. Bring those I contact to decision. Let me not be a milepost on a single road. Make me a fork that men must turn one way or another on facing the Christ in me."[17]

Awakening to the realization of how we can build upon previous generations entails both taking advantage of their progress and correcting the course to avoid their pitfalls.

Discipling the nations is the only strategy for fulfilling *The First Commission* and filling the earth with the glory of our God and His Christ!

---

[17] Jim Elliot, martyred missionary to Ecuador (1927-1956)

# Chapter 4
# FACING UP TO
# FELONIOUS FAILURES

I have heard dozens, maybe hundreds of messages on the Great Commission during my fifty years in the church.[1] But, I have yet to hear the first message on *The First Commission.* The eventual and ultimate fruit of obedience to *The First Commission* will be the kingdom of God on the earth as it is in heaven. The Great Commission is a functional strategy to that end.

> **Anything less than *the mind of Christ* will likely define the "church" as something less than what she is.**

I find it interesting that God did not instruct Adam and Eve to start a church or go to church. "Church"—those called out to be His family—had to wait for a *new creation* which would not appear on the scene for many years. The overview of God's *First Commission* to the first male and female was kingdom concentric.

What is a church? Is it a multi-million-dollar structure in an upscale suburb? Is it a simple mud brick structure with thatched roof and dirt floor? Does God live in temples made with men's hands? Or does He inhabit the living-stone-structure created in His image and likeness? The church of Christ is the temple of the living God, composed of human beings that believe in His Son, Jesus Christ. We are the Temple structure made without men's hands.

---

[1] If only evangelicalism had captured the wholeness and purpose of **The First Commission**, and realized that the gospel of the kingdom is far more-reaching than the gospel of personal salvation, we would be much farther along. The full gospel is all-inclusive. It is God-concentric, kingdom-concentric, not simply salvation concentric.

Anything less than *the mind of Christ*[2] will likely define the "church" as something less than what she is. The mind of Christ is ours as a result of being born spiritually as a new creation, and then being *transformed by the renewing of our minds*.[3]

Apart from Christ, in our old man, we are a felonious people by nature, repeating and compounding the mistakes of our forefathers. We are holding the gospel of the kingdom hostage by our failure to go back to the beginning and adjust our vision to the vision of our Father in heaven. His life in us = His vision for us.

The first felony of the twentieth century church was to replace *The First Commission*[4] with The Great Commission.[5] If *The First Commission* were being faithfully and obediently embraced, *The Great Commission* would be almost automatic!

Our second felony was to alter *The Great Commission*, robbing it of kingdom substance and eternal purpose.

"The Kingdom advances in the earth not through campaigns of moral, political, or social reformation, nor even church growth, but through the primary sign of its presence – Christ dwelling in the hearts of men."[6]

Jesus commands us to *disciple the nations*; we misinterpret that to mean *evangelize the nations*. Evangelism adds *numbers*; discipleship adds *workers—sons and daughters of the kingdom*[7] fully engaged in kingdom activity. Evangelism is made up of moments; discipleship is a lifestyle for both the teacher and the learner.

---

[2] 1 Corinthians 2:16
[3] Romans 12:1-2
[4] Genesis 1:27-28
[5] Matthew 28:19-20
[6] David Orton
[7] Matthew 13:38

36

A relatively small percentage of those who are evangelized become disciples.[8] The majority equates new birth to forgiveness of sins and eternal life—but there's more. Far more!

I still get emotional while watching reruns of Billy Graham Crusades or Oral Roberts Healing Revivals. The simplicity and holy power that operated in these two spiritual men and many others was breath-taking. So many people were changed forever through such ministries. They both had the wisdom to target fifth graders, and thereby appealed to the masses.

Undoubtedly, they did what they were called to do. We cannot lay at their feet the responsibility anymore than we can blame the delivery room doctor for failure to raise babies to maturity.

We have also met numerous people who were very positively blessed by a Sunday school teacher. Yet, we cannot blame those selfless servants for not growing up the kids in their classes. Nor can we make a legitimate argument for Sunday schools being responsible for training children. Read my lips: "Parenting!"

There would have been no second felony without the first felony! *The Great Commission* is a key strategy for fulfilling *The First Commission.* Failure to faithfully live out *The First Commission* generated the altering of *The Great Commission.*

*Behaving like mere men,*[9] most are totally unaware that these felonies have been committed. The church today continues with business as usual, not realizing that we have been called to *unusual business!* Few even realize that *The Great Commission* is directed to everyone numbered among the *royal priesthood* (all true believers).

---

[8] Dave Shirkey identifies these three elements as necessary in comprehensive discipleship:  TEACHING (which involves a subject and results in increased knowledge), TRAINING (which involves a task and results in increased skill), and EQUIPPING (which involves a person and results in increased capacity).
[9] 1 Corinthians 3:3

Many wrongly believe that *The Great Commission* is intended for the religious professionals—a third felony! This is actually two felonies in one: (1) that *The Great Commission* applies only to religious professionals, and (2) that there are to be religious professionals in the church. Neither concept is supported by New Covenant Scripture.

- Leaders? Yes.
- Shepherds? Yes.
- Equipping servants? Yes.
- A separate class of elite professionals? No! [10]

I was once a part of an "apostolic network" that catered to "an elite class of professionals" in exchange for their tithes. I'm so sorry! We didn't see it and would not have described it in such crass terms.

Dwight Pentecost said, "Some of the greatest satanic activity in the end times will take place in the pulpit."

We should be very slow and cautious about judging motives and sincerity. Many are brothers and sisters who have been gifted, discipled, anointed and placed in our midst for our edification and maturation. Most are simply following the patterns and procedures of previous generations. Some are undoubtedly "wolves."

*God's Purpose* is the victim of these felonies.

*The First Commission* is our vision; *The Great Commission*[11] is our strategy. Both are to dynamically involve every believer born of God! We are a *kingdom of priests*[12]—*a royal priesthood.*[13]

Israel's fruitlessness caused the kingdom to be taken from them, to be *given to a nation that bears the fruit* of the kingdom.[14]  Peter

---

[11] To disciple the nations
[12] Exodus 19:6
[13] 1 Peter 2:2:9
[14] Matthew 21:43

speaks of *a holy nation*.[15] John explains that this holy nation is to be made up of people out of *every tribe and tongue and people and nation*, having made us (to be) *a kingdom of priests—a royal priesthood, a holy nation*.[16]

The presumption of the masses is that their purpose is to evangelize those within their spheres of influence, and financially support the "professionals." Only a very small percentage of church members actually live up to these presumptions. Many are vaguely aware of a coming kingdom, believing it to be in heaven sometime in the very distant future. Even the years and years of praying for *the kingdom to come on the earth* has not penetrated, or produced faith for our time in history. People pray it by rote, but don't have a living faith for it to really happen. Such prayers are without faith and are not heard in heaven.

Jentezen Franklin says, "We were not created to be church furniture!"

Missing *The First Commission* unfortunately results in missing the motivation, essence and substance of *The Great Commission* and creates *an audience culture of spiritual wimps.* Longevity is wrongly believed to produce maturity. And comfort zones are defined in terms of tradition's ruts.

May we open our hearts and eyes to a purpose-filled life that is consistent with *The First Commission*.

> *So God created man in His own image; in the image of God He created him; male and female He created them.*
>
> *Then God blessed them, and God said to them, "Be fruitful and multiply; fill the earth and subdue it; have dominion over the fish of the sea, over the birds of the air, and over every living thing that moves on the earth."*[17]

---

[15] 1 Peter 2:9
[16] Revelation 5:9-10
[17] Genesis 1:27-28

1. Be fruitful
2. Multiply
3. Fill the Earth
4. Subdue it
5. Reign

*"The kingdom of God will be given to a nation bearing the fruits of it."*

# Chapter 5
# BIRDS, BEES AND KINGDOM INTENTIONS

"God's government in his Son was conceived in the heart of the Father before time began. This has implications in how we approach God and our mission in the world."[1]

> *Your wife shall be like a fruitful vine in the very heart of your house, your children like olive plants all around your table.*[2]

> **Dare we put our minds to rest cradled within His will?**

This would be a scary thought in present-day culture of twin bathtubs on the waterfront, and birth control available to children with neither a prescription nor parental consent required. The thought of *children like olive plants all around your table* would certainly conflict those with self-centered career plans!

Can we praise our way through this cultural fog and allow the light of God to adjust our thinking? Dare we put our minds to rest cradled within His will? Dare we?

> *He created them male and female, and blessed them and called them Mankind in the day they were created.*[3]

God made no mistake in the specificity of His creation, perfectly designed to fulfill His eternal intention in fellowship with Him. He designed them to be *male and female*. He created them *male and female*. He blessed them *male and female*.

---

[1] David Orton
[2] Psalm 128:3
[3] Genesis 5:2

A recent advertisement for children's shoes featured a princess of a little girl all frilly and feminine, and a roughneck boy exercising unchecked masculinity. The caption for the girl was: "Pretty!" The caption for the boy: "Power."

Can you believe it? There is now organized opposition to the ad, charging that it unfairly stereotypes these children. Get serious!

God created a man and a woman, the foundation for a family, with the ability to be fruitful and multiply—thus initiating a growing family that, through the generations would fill the earth with His kingdom and glory. God has not changed His mind. He is so intentional in this matter that He prophetically promises a latter day redemptive period:

> *"Behold, I will send you Elijah the prophet before the coming of the great and dreadful day of the Lord. And he will turn the hearts of fathers to the children, and the hearts of children to their fathers, lest I come and strike the earth with a curse."*[4]

There are so many who have given much of their adult lives to finding their absentee fathers. And also many fathers invest everything they have to locate their children, Many have no idea that this is a "God thing." They just know that there will be no peace within unless and until this link is restored.

This book is about God's family filling, subduing and reigning in the earth through faithful obedience to the Holy Spirit and *The First Commission.*

> *However, the spiritual is not first, but the natural, and afterward the spiritual.*[5]

---

[4] Malachi 4:5-6
[5] 1 Corinthians 15:46

The restoration of natural links will round off mountains and fill in valleys for so many people—fathers and children alike. Where impossible, we may still discover our wholeness through adoption:

> *For we did not receive the spirit of bondage again to fear, but you received the Spirit of adoption by whom we cry out, "Abba, Father."*

> *The Spirit Himself bears witness with our spirit that we are children of God, and if children, then heirs—heirs of God and joint heirs with Christ.*[6]

Nature specifically confirms that it is God's will for women—mothers--to *bring forth* children with the help of men—fathers. Scripture specifically confirms that it is God's will for men—fathers—to *bring up* children with the help of women—mothers.

> *And you, fathers, do not provoke your children to wrath, but bring them up in the training and admonition of the Lord.*[7]

Every child should be the benefactor of two parents uniquely joined as one, and able to help that child find the answers to these questions:

- Who am I?
- Where did I come from?
- Why am I here?
- What can I do?
- Where am I going?

Normal godly fathering helps children find the answers to these gripping questions. What I am saying here would seem far from normal in today's culture. Many adults have no answers to the above questions, much less any way of helping their children to

---

[6] Romans 8:15-17a
[7] Ephesians 6:4

find such answers. No matter how old one gets, he/she is yet immature and ill-equipped without answers to these questions.

Some spend their lifetimes creating answers to these questions for themselves with varying levels futility. Many turn to artificial stimuli such as alcohol, drugs, infidelity, etc., to keep it together and to prepare them for another day on the hamster treadmill.

Perhaps you are having difficulty with the idea of fathers having a lead role in bringing up children. I will admit that this might seem quite dogmatic if it is without the context of a rightly ordered marriage that results in two people becoming one flesh, and fleshing out that order within that oneness.

Let me ask you a simple question: Would you object to Jesus having the lead role and His bride as His helper?

There undoubtedly will be those who remind me that all metaphors are limited in application. So, let me ask the question in this way:

Would you object to the church having the leading role and Jesus being her helper?

I invite you to use the same application insofar as this particular metaphor is concerned. I would also offer that this just might not be a metaphor. Perhaps this is a revealing of *a great mystery*.[8] I believe that it is, and appeal to you for your prayerful consideration (and/or reconsideration).

There has never been a time in history when it was more challenging for God to *set the solitary into families*. Based upon current statistical percentages, there are more individuals without families and fewer solid godly families who are ready, willing and able to assimilate the solitary.

Apart from *The First Commission* and revelation of God's purpose in it, humanity automatically devalues life by existing apart from

---

[8] Ephesians 5:32

44

divine purpose and provision. Exponential increase of murders and suicides confirm this spiraling devaluation. Our culture has lost any sense of personal responsibility and consequences for our actions. People do not understand that death is not the end of the matter.

Statistics make it clear that attempted suicide is a big deal as it relates to the youth. It is the third leading cause of death for teenagers. Males are four times more likely to die from suicide than females. However, teen girls are more likely than teen boys to attempt suicide."[9]

Convoluted and corrupt cultures are largely the fruit of fatherless homes and societies. God's father-heart is made known from creation through redemption and even in the way that we were taught to pray (to "Our Father"). Correction to the world's ills is wrapped in returning to and fulfilling *The First Commission.*

> *Correct your son, and he will give you rest; yes, he will give delight to your heart. Where there is not vision [no redemptive revelation of God], the people perish; but he who keeps the law [of God, which includes that of man]— blessed (happy, fortunate, and enviable) is he.*[10]

Every vision needs visionaries willing to follow the cause. Commitment, energy, enthusiasm, giftedness—the things visions are made of—all should direct our focus to the tree of life in the midst of the garden of God. Christ is our cause!

> *In the beginning was the Word, and the Word was with God, and* ***the Word was God.*** *He was in the beginning with God. All things were made through Him, and without Him nothing was made that was made. In Him was life, and the life was the light of man.*[11]

---

[9] Excerpts from: www.teensuicide.us
[10] Proverbs 29:17-18 AMP
[11] John 1:1-4

*And **the Word became flesh** and dwelt among us, and we beheld His glory, the glory as of the only begotten of the Father, full of grace and truth.*[12]

This brings us to a fourth felony. Some have replaced the Person of Christ with the Scriptures. He came in the Person of His Son by virtue of the Holy Spirit to abide in you Himself!

*For **the word of God is living** and powerful and sharper than any two-edged sword, piercing even to the division of soul and spirit, and of joints and marrow, and is a discerner of the thoughts and intents of the heart. And there is no creature hidden from **His sight**, but all things are naked and open to the eyes of Him to whom we must give an account.*[13]

Dr. Stephen Crosby states: "The Bible is like a resume: factually accurate, but not the same as actually meeting the Person it represents."

Thomas Manton says: "In the Scriptures there is a portrait of God, but in Christ there is God Himself. A coin bears the image of Caesar, but Caesar's son is his own lively resemblance. Christ is the living Bible."

The Anointed One, *Christ in us, the hope of glory,*[14] has already paid the price to redeem us from these felonies as well as all sin, and granted us new life in relationship with His Spirit. He can also envision, lead and empower His new creation on the mission to right these historical wrongs.

*Listen to your father who begot you, and do not despise your mother when she is old. Buy the truth, and do not sell it, also wisdom and instruction and understanding.*[15]

---

[12] John 1:14
[13] Hebrews 4:12-13
[14] Colossians 1:27
[15] Proverbs 23:22-23

# Chapter 6
# CORRUPTED AND CONVOLUTED CULTURES

It is the dreams, visions and creative thinking of fallen mankind that corrupts and convolutes cultures.

For example, the issues with Congress and the Administration—even the Supreme Court of the United States—are the fruit of the culture that sent them to Washington. In truth, they are accurate representatives of their constituency. Their speech is confounded and confounding. They cannot hear or understand one another.

> *At one time, the whole Earth spoke the same language. It so happened that as they moved out of the east they came upon a plain in the land of Shinar and settled down.*

**The spirits of this age—individualism and independence—have overtaken a people created to find expression for their individuality within the context of interdependently relating members of the body of Christ.**

*They said to one another, "Come, let's make brick and fire them well." They used brick for stone and tar for mortar.*

Don't simply overlook these decisions and substitutions. Jesus contrasted the *wise man* who built his house on *rock* and the *foolish man* who built his house on *sand*. We saw in India that their bricks may be made from mud, but their foundations are granite hewn in the quarry, placed together with mortar.

The granite foundations for major structures in India are set in place for an absolute minimum of one year before anything is built upon them—before they bear any weight. Yet, the church promotes people based upon their charismatic personalities and talents. Could this be an important metaphor? Why would the Scripture make this contrast of *brick for stone and tar for mortar?*

> *Then they said, "Come, let's build ourselves a city and a tower that reaches Heaven. Let's make ourselves famous so we won't be scattered here and there across the Earth."*

It never occurred to them that the God of Abraham, Isaac and Jacob may have intended for them to *be scattered here and there across the Earth.* In fact, that is what eventually happened, only not for the cause of the kingdom as He would have designed. But their hearts were to settle down in that which was familiar and comfortable, and build monuments to themselves.

> *God came down to look over the city and the tower those people had built. God took one look and said, "One people, one language; why, this is only a first step. No telling what they'll come up with next—they'll stop at nothing!"*

God knows our frame and what we are capable of. He—Father, Son and Holy Spirit existing in oneness—is totally aware of the power of agreement.

> *"Come, we'll go down and garble their speech so they won't understand each other." Then God scattered them from there all over the world. And they had to quit building the city. That's how it came to be called Babel, because there God turned their language into "babble." From there God scattered them all over the world.[1]*

It is interesting to note that God poured out the Spirit of His Son on all flesh when *there were dwelling in Jerusalem Jews, devout men,*

---

[1] Genesis 11:1-9 TM

48

*from every nation under heaven.*[2]  As Peter and the others began, *everyone heard them speak in his own language.*[3]

Our own pride, desires and ambitions hinder us from hearing one another.  Humanly speaking, we are denominated when a number of people come into agreement around sectarian ideas, treating our parts as though they were the whole.

The whole is greater than any part thereof.

Yielding to Jesus as Lord and being led by His Spirit will gradually bring us back into loving oneness and the ability to hear one another.

The culture war that rages on Capitol Hill and at 1600 Pennsylvania Avenue NW is fueled by the demands and expectations of a widely diverse voting public.  We could boil down the corporate language of Americans to "babble."

It's not so much about Republican and Democrats, Conservatives and Liberals.  It is about metaphorical "kingdom building" with bricks and tar, laboring for self-interests from very different perspectives, with very different values.

*The salt of the earth* has lost its flavor and, been rendered *good for nothing*, it is being *trampled underfoot by men. The light of the world* that is to be the bride city set on a hill has been subdivided into a few candles here and several candles there—some red, some blue, some short and fat and others tall and thin, none resembling the Template by whom we were made.

Communities created to serve now expect to be served; creators created to create have caved to consumerism competing for market shares. The spirits of this age—individualism and independence— have overtaken a people created to find expression for their

---

[2] Acts 2:5
[3] Acts 2:6

individuality within the context of interdependently relating members of the body of Christ.

The distinctives of kingdom culture cannot be resurrected because we all speak different languages. We all have different ideals and goals and objectives. We have become in large measure what we have been created to overcome—Babylon!

(This is just the fifth chapter, not the last chapter!)

Let's just consider one example of conflict that has convoluted and corrupted culture.

The radical changing of priorities that affected lives during and immediately following World War II created new levels of selfishness, self-indulgence that essentially closed the door on absolutes and opened door for situational ethics and all that has come with the age of enlightenment.

Women were discovering a whole new world of opportunities and possibilities that were previously beyond the natural and normal boundaries of homemaking at that time in history. The emerging of concerns about women's rights was also fed by dogmatic stereotypes regarding gender roles.

Compounding sixty-five years of gradual changes since then, we should not be surprised by the evolution away from homemaking. Now, even motherhood is being rejected!

The August 12, 2013, edition of Time Magazine's cover photo is intended to glorify "The Childfree Life." The copy line: "When having it all means not having children." The Index uses the title, "The Cons of Procreation." And, the first page declares: "NONE IS ENOUGH."[4]

The birthrate in the U. S. is the lowest in recorded American history, which includes the fertility crash of the Great Depression.

---

[4] By Lauren Sandler

From 2007 to 2011, the most recent years for which there is data, the fertility rate declined 9%. One in five women now end their childbearing age childless, up from one in ten in the 1970's.

Are these role models? (Notable Non-Moms)

Gloria Steinem: "I'm completely happy not having children. I mean, everybody does not have to live in the same way. And as somebody said, 'Everybody with a womb doesn't have to have a child any more than everybody with vocal cords has to be an opera singer.'"

Margaret Cho: "Babies scare me more than anything."

Oprah Winfrey: "I have none—not one regret about not having children—because I believe that it is the way it's supposed to be."

Dolly Parton: "My songs are like my children—I expect them to support me when I'm old."

Katharine Hepburn: "I had such a wonderful upbringing that I had a very high standard of how a mother and father should behave. I couldn't be that way and carry on a movie career."

Condoleezza Rice: "I'm very religious, and I at some very deep level believe that things are going to work out as they're supposed to. The key is to be open to that and to appreciate the life that you've been given."

Janet Jackson: "It would be very, very sweet if I did have children, the icing on the cake. And I like sweet things. But it doesn't feel essential."

A report released this week by AARP projects that by 2030 there will be only 4 potential caregivers available for each person 80 or older, down from 7 in 2010. By 2050, when baby boomers are between 86 and 104, the ratio will drop below 3 to 1.

Will this not add another layer of sound reasoning for considering Euthanasia? Go figure!

In a December column[5] in the New York Times, Ross Douthat argued that the "retreat from child rearing is, at some level, a symptom of late-modern exhaustion"—an indicator of "decadence," revealing "a spirit that privileges the present over the future." (Would this be anything like putting our grandchildren into debt?)

Ross nailed it: "a spirit that privileges the present over the future." This spirit is driving the corrupting and convoluting of a culture that for many years was influenced by *"the light of the world. A city (within cities) that is set on a hill"*[6]

Such a city must be guided and enabled, not by a spirit that privileges the present over the past, but by a spirit that sacrifices the present in favor of the future. The choice is *irresponsible living or living responsibly.* Do we care more about ourselves than our grandchildren and their children's children?

Some are *eating their seed* without understanding *The First Commission*, and without caring that there will be no *progeny.* "Let the other guy do it! I've got my career to take care of!" Well, so does "the other guy." What is God's will?

"Be fruitful and multiply!"

> *Now may He who supplies seed to the sower, and bread for food, supply and multiply the seed you have sown and increase the fruits of your righteousness . . .*[7]

So many do not know the difference between seed to sow and bread to eat! They are eating their seed!

---

[5] "More Babies, Please"
[6] Matthew 5:14
[7] 2 Corinthians 9:10

*And Judah said to Onan, "Go in to your brother's wife and marry her, and raise up an heir to your brother." But Onan knew that the heir would not be his; and it came to pass, when he went in to his brother's wife, that he emitted on the ground, lest he should give an heir to his brother.*

*And the thing which he did displeased the Lord . . .*[8]

*The First Commission: "Be fruitful and multiply."* God is displeased when anyone eats the seed that is provided for sowing, or when anyone spills his seed on the ground!

I am not saying that all women under all circumstances should bear children. What I am challenging is the present-day antichrist culture that is more than neutral in its influence. Here is a little history regarding degeneracy of godless cultures as it pertains to our subject:

"Religious adherents vary widely in their views on birth control. This can be true even between different branches of one faith, as in the case of Judaism. Some religious believers find that their own opinions of the use of birth control differ from the beliefs espoused by the leaders of their faith, and many grapple with the ethical dilemma of what is perceived as "correct action" according to their faith, versus personal circumstance, reason, and choice.

"Among Christian denominations today there are a large variety of positions towards contraception. The Roman Catholic Church has disallowed artificial contraception for as far back as one can historically trace. Contraception was also officially disallowed by non-Catholic Christians until 1930 when the Anglican Communion changed its policy. Soon after, most Protestant groups came to accept the use of modern contraceptives as a matter of Biblically allowable freedom of conscience."[9]

---

[8] Genesis 38:8-10a
[9] Wikipedia

Woman who claim the right to choose would do well to compare their own prejudices and preferences with the eternal purpose of God to see if they are aligned to please Him.

Those of us in the new creation, who are being led by the Holy Spirit can trust our interactive consciences to answer these questions for us. It is good to ask questions so that we might find the general will of God, then hold it up against our consciences as a bride making decisions together with our husbands and Husband.

To determine that "none is enough" without such processing is diametrically against our Creator and Savior, who said: *"Be fruitful, multiply and fill the earth."* It is a total denial of *The First Commission.*

To arrive at such conclusions and make such decisions casually without prayerfully seeking God's will in one's specific extreme is—what was the word that Ross Douthat used?—"decadent," as those who *have changed the glory of the incorruptible God into an image made like corruptible man . . . who exchange the truth of God for the lie, and worshiped and served the creature rather than the Creator.*[10]

You know where this conversation inevitably goes.

But, let's have another conversation. Let's suppose that we could just take God at His word, dig our spiritual heels in, and get to the root of the problem. There is life for us in the words of the prophet Isaiah:

> *Arise, shine; for your light has come! And the glory of the Lord is risen upon you.*
>
> *For behold, the darkness shall cover the earth, and deep darkness the people; but the Lord will arise over you, and His glory will be seen upon you.*[11]

---

[10] Romans 1:22-25
[11] Isaiah 60:1-2

# Chapter 7
# WORLD WAR II AND
# THE *CULTURE WAR*

December 7, 1941, was a particularly traumatic day for a six-year-old. Mom and the woman next door were desperately clinging to one another, trembling, and crying their eyes out. Something was terribly wrong. And this six-year-old could only grasp the trauma of the moment and remember it for a lifetime.

I would later begin to understand the torment that engulfed my mother and our neighbor. The Japanese had bombed Pearl Harbor, the United States had officially declared war, and wives and mothers throughout the land shared the relentless fear that their husbands would be drafted into military service, and—who knows?

> Imagine a culture in which you could trust your little children to safely go on a streetcar and to a theater alone!

Food was *not* rationed in the US during the Great Depression. Many people had difficulty buying it, but the government did not impose rationing until the need arose to send large quantities of food overseas to the armed forces during World War 2. I remember Dad trading ration stamps for liquor and tobacco for meat stamps and other foods. Dad was always a good provider, thrifty, doing whatever was necessary to be responsible. (What a heritage!)

Realizing that my world back then was quite small and my perspective very limited, there are some very real experiences that can be pieced together as parts of the same puzzle. Retrospect, hindsight, is said to be 20/20 vision.

It wasn't long until things really began to change. For many, it was men going to war and women going to work. Dad never was drafted, but Mom did go to work in a war factory, working nights and sleeping days while Dad worked days and slept nights.

Being the oldest, with two younger brothers, household management became a part of my young life. There were no daycare centers. Besides, either Dad or Mom was in the house. All I can tell you is that life was different. Culture was under attack. And, I've lived long enough to see the fruit.

I remember Mom and several other ladies began smoking— unheard of in our culture up to that time. Mom's world was larger; mine was simply different. It even smelled different. But, there was an upside.

A quarter—twenty-five cents allowance each Saturday made it possible for me to afford a round-trip streetcar ticket (ten cents), a ticket to the matinee (ten cents) and a nickel (five cents) for popcorn. There was a newsreel (boring), a comic strip (funny) and a serial (compelling) as well as a full-length movie—usually a western!

Imagine a culture in which you could trust your little children to safely go on a streetcar and to a theater alone! That contrast alone, from the mid-1940s to the present, should get our attention. It so represents the two different worlds that I have lived in. I did not need to go to a different nation. A different nation came to me!

I remember a family trip into downtown Cleveland where we joined a crowd of people standing on the sidewalk staring into a storefront window. This was our first time to see television! The seven-inch screen was filled with "snow" and some vague figures and activity in black and white. We were amazed with this new technology!

You would consider it "amazing" if your lifelong experience to date had been running in from school and flopping down on the living-room floor to listen to several back-to-back fifteen-minute serials on the floor-model radio. The Phantom, Batman and Robin, The Lone Ranger, Superman, Terry and the Pirates (not a ball team from Pittsburgh), Captain Marvel. I could go on and on. And, why wouldn't anyone want to eat Wheaties, "the breakfast of champions?"

It wasn't long until our next-door neighbors got the first TV in our neighborhood and opened their doors to all for the Friday night fights. Sponsored by Gillette, they started at 10:00 p.m. We tried to get there at 9:30 to gaze at the "test pattern" on the screen for a half hour. (You must understand that this was the latest technology for our generation!)

Many women were working, smoking and even wearing pants! The old way of clarifying family order by who was *wearing the pants in the family* became obsolete.

Not only was culture significantly affected by role confusion regarding moms, dads[12]—those who hadn't gone to war and those returning from war found themselves in a post-depression culture that afforded many new financial opportunities. Wages increased and overtime rode the wave of economic plenty because of wartime production and fewer men in the workforce. Allowances for children increased many-fold from that quarter per week all the way to paper money.

Of course, prices also were on the rise. No longer could you get a "shave and a haircut for two bits (twenty-five cents)." Those who survived the Great Depression and World War II, and subsequently found themselves living the American dream in a land of plenty were set up for a major cultural shift.

As men returned from military service to the waiting arms and hearts of their wives, the "baby boom" generation came into being.

Male + Female = Fruitfulness/Multiplication.

---

[12] This would eventually lead to role confusion between "male and female" and all that comes with it.

Baby boomers are associated with a rejection or redefinition of traditional values, many of which were biblical values deeply rooted in the culture of the older generation.

**Narcissism** is a term that originated with Narcissus in Greek mythology who fell in love with his own image reflected in a pool of water. Currently it is used to describe a person characterized by egotism, vanity, pride, or selfishness.[13]

*The Culture of Narcissism: American Life in an Age of Diminishing Expectations* is a book by the cultural historian Christopher Lasch, first published in January 1979. It explores the roots and ramifications of the normalizing of pathological narcissism in 20th century American culture using psychological, cultural, artistic and historical synthesis.[14]

Other writers have captured the degree and nature of this psychological and pathological cultural "disease" with titles such as *Malignant Narcissism* and *The Narcissism Epidemic.*

Narcissism in those days would compare to the developing freedoms of the growing gay communities in these days—without the legal and moral issues. Although narcissism did not get any "press," it has had a far more universal effect on culture.

It is at the root of America's problems. Narcissism encompasses self-centeredness, selfishness, greed and more. It has infected Washington, D. C., and every community that has elected this representative government. Democracy may not survive much longer.

In 1887 Alexander Tyler, a Scottish history professor at the University of Edinburgh, had this to say about the fall of the Athenian Republic some 2,000 years prior: "A democracy is always temporary in nature; it simply cannot exist as a permanent form of government. A democracy will continue to

---

13 Wikipedia
14 Wikipedia

58

exist up until the time that voters discover that they can vote themselves generous gifts from the public treasury. From that moment on, the majority always votes for the candidates who promise the most benefits from the public treasury, with the result that every democracy will finally collapse over loose fiscal policy, (which is) always followed by a dictatorship."[15]

"The average age of the world's greatest civilizations from the beginning of history, has been about 200 years. During those 200 years, these nations always progressed through the following sequence:

> From bondage to spiritual faith;
> From spiritual faith to great courage;
> From courage to liberty;
> From liberty to abundance;
> From abundance to complacency;
> From complacency to apathy;
> From apathy to dependence;
> From dependence back into bondage."

Surely the demographics of the USA track with these observations. I have lived through the process. A subtitle for an article in the latest "Barna Update" reads:

> "The Longer Hispanics Experience U.S. Culture,
> The Less Socially Conservative they Become"

People infect cultures, and cultures infect people. This does not happen instantly. The sowing of seeds—good and bad— may happen quickly; but it takes a process of seasons for full fruition.

Barbara and I met in junior high school in the days immediately post World War II. We were married in 1954, and raised our family during the most radical years of cultural deterioration.

---

[15] The national debt is nearing seventeen-trillion dollars and has continued to increase an average of $2.07 billion per day since September 30, 2012!

I remember one daughter cutting high school English classes because the teacher was teaching Transcendental Meditation. Another daughter left a science class in which the teacher had the class write as many "street expressions" describing the various parts of the human anatomy. He also displayed a picture of a pregnant male. This was in the late 1970s! "As California goes, so goes the nation—eventually." Both girls opted to go for their GED.

We managed to pass on to our children the virtues and values in which we were raised. It takes multiple generations for cultures to be completely changed to the point that the younger people cannot even relate to such antiquated values. That would describe our grandchildren who are now raising their children, our great-grandchildren, in an entirely different worldview and culture than we knew.

The precursor to all that is available today for diagnosing and prescribing how to live the ultimate self life was *Psychology Today,* founded in 1967. It is still published six times a year and features articles on such topics as love, relationships, sex, happiness, success, depression, and self-empowerment.

This list of features sounds very much like the agendas of many churches which are trying to meet people where they are, and incorporate the gospel in with sincere efforts to provide practical help.

We have watched with dismay the manipulative catering to narcissistic appetites by Hollywood and Madison Avenue.

> *For all that is in the world—the lust of the flesh, the lust of the eyes, and the pride of life—is not of the Father but is of the world. And the world is passing away, and the lusts of it; but he who does the will of God abides forever.*[16]

---

[16] 1 John 2:16-17

# Chapter 8
# KINGDOM CULTURE
# AND A NEW CREATION

There is a kingdom culture!

Antichrist cultures are nurtured in *gray areas*. Most would fear to tread where there is total darkness. A little light affords opportunities for denigration to chip away at righteousness without being noticed except by the most discerning and mature in spiritual understanding— those who actually *walk in the light*. Babies see light and shadows long before walking in light and substance. Perhaps demons, like bats, tend to sleep during the full light of day.

> The new creation, born of God's Spirit, is enabled to grow into God's mysterious wisdom and discern His divine intent.

The caretakers of compromise point to the little light they have to justify their ignorance concerning purpose and intent. The blind of spirit lead the blind of spirit, supposing that the outer limits of their selfish desires represent the ultimate in life. They falter and fall together, headlong, hand-in-hand into the proverbial ditch because their backs are to what little light they have, and their own shadows hide the edge of the eternal abyss from their view.

> *Refusing to know God, they soon didn't know how to be human either—women didn't know how to be women, men didn't know how to be men. Sexually confused, they abused and defiled one another, women with women, men with men—all lust, no love.*[1]

---

[1] Romans 1:26-27 TM

For a man to desire another man is unnatural. For a woman to desire another woman is unnatural. For a man to not desire fatherhood is unnatural. For a woman to not desire motherhood is unnatural.[2]

Passing legislation does not affect the lighting. Unfortunately, here in the United States, there is no longer enough light to affect legislation.

> *For this you know, that no fornicator, unclean person, nor covetous man, who is an idolater, has any inheritance in the kingdom of Christ and God. Let no one deceive you with empty words, for because of these things the wrath of God comes upon the sons of disobedience. Therefore do not be partakers with them.*
>
> *For you were once darkness, but now you are light in the Lord. Walk as children of the light (for the fruit of the Spirit is in all goodness, righteousness, and truth), finding out what is acceptable to the Lord.*
>
> *And have no fellowship with the unfruitful works of darkness, but rather expose them. For it is shameful even to speak of these things which are done by them in secret. But all things that are exposed are made manifest by the light, for whatever makes manifest is light.[3]*

For the church to regain our bearings will require (1) affirming the demarcation that separates soul and spirit (the breath of God), (2) a return to the essential nature of our creation, and (3) a clear understanding of and faithful obedience to *The First Commission*:

1. *The Lord God . . . breathed into his nostrils the breath of life.*

2. *Male and female created He them.*

---

[2] Below God's intention—subnormal by God's standard
[3] Ephesians 5:8-13

3.  *Then God blessed them, and God said to them, "Be fruitful and multiply."*

This is in Genesis, the history of creation and intention. Purpose is defined in original intention. Unless and until our points of reference are consistent with the divine intention in creation, the shadows of our own being can trip us up and do us in.

The last verse of the first chapter of Genesis states:

> *Then God saw everything that He had made, and indeed it was very good.*

How can we improve on what God sees and calls *very good*?

> *God's wisdom is something mysterious that goes deep into the interior of His purpose. You don't find it lying around on the surface. It's not the latest message, but more like the oldest—what God determined as the way to bring out His best in us, long before we ever arrived on the scene. The experts of our day haven't a clue about what this eternal plan is.*[4]

The new creation,[5] born of God's Spirit,[6] is enabled to grow into God's mysterious wisdom and discern His divine intent, beginning by considering the brief insights offered just prior to the first serpentine intervention.

Beginning with the largest of big pictures, we see that *the heavens and the earth, and all the host of them were finished* at the same time.[7] It is reasonable to believe that there was no separation between the heavens and the earth, that the interests, intents and divine characteristics of heaven were inherent within earth's creation.

---

[4] 1 Corinthians 2:6-7 TM
[5] 2 Corinthians 5:17
[6] John 3:3-8
[7] Genesis 2:1

God walked in the garden—where He had placed Adam and Eve—in the cool of the day. There was no separation between God and His creation. Jesus spoke of a return to that status of togetherness with Him and with one another in Christ:

- *"Lo, I am with you always, even to the end of the age."*[8]

- *And they went out and preached everywhere, the Lord working with them and confirming the word through the accompanying signs.*[9]

- *"Behold, I send the Promise of My Father upon you; but tarry in the city of Jerusalem until you are endued with power from on high."*[10]

- *"I will not leave you orphans; I will come to you."*[11]

Paul, the benefactor of an experiential new covenant grace, wrote:

- *If then you were raised with Christ, seek those things which are above, where Christ is, sitting at the right hand of God.*

- *Set your mind on things above, not on things on the earth.*

- *For you died, and your life is hidden with Christ in God.*

- *When Christ who is our life appears, then you also will appear with Him in glory.*[12]

Following Adam and Eve's independent actions of disobedience, God barred them from the garden. Suddenly, for them, the heavens were higher than the earth. And God's thoughts and ways were higher than their thoughts and ways.[13] The forbidden fruit of

---

[8] Matthew 28:20
[9] Mark 16:20
[10] Luke 24:49
[11] John 14:18
[12] Colossians 3:1-4

*the tree of the knowledge of good and evil* dictated their thoughts and ways. Deprived of life in the Spirit, they became earthbound—the condition in which we all were until *light* came and we were born again of His Spirit.

> *This is the history of the heavens and the earth when they were created, in the same day that the Lord God made the earth and the heavens.*[14]

The reconciling of the heavens and the earth is significant to the new creation:

> *Now all things are of God, who has reconciled us to Himself through Jesus Christ, and has given us the ministry of reconciliation.*[15]

> *(God) made us alive together with Christ, and raised us up together, and made us sit together in the heavenly places in Christ Jesus.*[16]

Meanwhile, back in Genesis before that damning fruit-tasting event,

- *The Lord God formed man of the dust of the ground, and breathed into his nostrils the breath of life.*[17]

- *Then the Lord God took the man and put him in the garden of Eden to tend and keep it.*[18]

- *And the Lord God said, "It is not good that man should be alone; I will make him a helper comparable to him."*[19]

---

[13] Isaiah 55:8-9
[14] Genesis 2:4
[15] 2 Corinthians 5:18
[16] Ephesians 2:5-6
[17] Genesis 2:7
[18] Genesis 2:15
[19] Genesis 2:18

God would likely be labeled "male chauvinist" by many "liberated women" and compassionate men who have taken offense for these kinds of statements:

- *It is not good that man should be alone*
- *I will make him*
- *A helper*

God also said that Eve would be *comparable to Adam.* Differing roles do not necessarily mean differing values. Aren't you glad that you don't have to pit the members of your physical body against one another for relative value? Aren't you also glad that each has a purpose all of its own, and that we actually exist and function for the common good—in wholeness? Similarly,

> *The manifestation of the Spirit is given to each one for the profit of all.*[20]

Remember that these words were spoken before the "fall" and before there was any *culture* to blame for something that we choose not to believe.

I have had one wife for nearly sixty years. We together have raised four daughters. My wife has authored a book, co-authored another, written many articles, and has spoken to thousands in India. She and I are one, and we flow together without problem or issue. Our daughters are all successful as godly women. I have no bone to pick, only a testimony to share!

Is it not reasonable to believe that the fullness of fulfillment is ours in Christ as we align ourselves with His will, intent, and order, and walk out our purpose in faith? Is Love going to be less than what we need for fulfillment?

> *We continue to shout our praise even when we're hemmed in with troubles, because we know how troubles can develop passionate patience in us, and how that patience in*

---

[20] 1 Corinthians 12:7

*turn forges the tempered steel of virtue, keeping us alert for whatever God will do next. In alert expectancy such as this, we're never left feeling shortchanged. Quite the contrary—we can't round up enough containers to hold everything God generously pours into our lives through the Holy Spirit.*[21]

"Divine Alignment is more than just a divine pattern, but is God's Order in Right Relationships. You may have Divine Gifting but may not be in Alignment for His Divine Assignment. If not Divinely Aligned, there arises the Potentiality of being Malignant Mal - Align to the voice of the Lord and His calling for your LIFE. Become Aligned as the Lord Assigns you through Right Relationships for your life. For you desire God Vertically you will at some time in your life connect with Him Horizontally, Divine Relationships ordained of the Lord and your steps ordered thereof."[22]

Does not nature teach us? If your left arm was located in the place of your right leg, and your right leg was in the place of your left arm, you would considered "a freak of nature," not able to properly function.

We are like puzzle pieces, irregular in size and shape, but being shaped to fit together into a spiritual house, the dwelling place of God. When we all are mature and complete, functioning in the oneness and unction of His Spirit, we—together—will look just like Jesus!

This will be so in every locality in the world, a new creation on display for the glory of our Maker. All will see that Love's perfect will (government/kingdom) is worthy of our submission.

*God has highly exalted Him and given Him the name which is above every name, that at the name of Jesus every knee should bow, of those in heaven, and of those on earth, and*

---

[21] Romans 5:3-5 TM
[22] Timothy Early

*of those under the earth, and that every tongue should confess that Jesus Christ is Lord, to the glory of God the Father.*[23]

*I want you to know that the head of every man is Christ, the head of woman is man, and the head of Christ is God.*[24]

Have you ever given much thought to the truth that *the head of Christ is God*? Perhaps you have never fussed over Christ being the head of man. It just seems so natural. And, it seems to work fine. We know what a mess man can make of his life by not honoring Christ as his head.

To the extent that we discover God's order we experience His peace.[25] There is even specific order within the oneness of the Godhead!

Jesus said, *"The Son can do nothing of Himself, but what He sees the Father do; for whatever He does, the Son also does in like manner.*[26]

Jesus said of the Holy Spirit, *"He will not speak on His own authority, but whatever He hears He will speak; and He will tell you things to come. He will glorify Me, for He will take of what is Mine and declare it to you."*[27]

He also told His disciples, *"Do you not believe that I am in the Father, and the Father is in Me? The words that I speak to you I do not speak on My own authority; but the Father who dwells in Me does the works."*[28] The Son is the glory of the Father. The Holy Spirit reveals the Son. God is bringing many sons to glory. Woman is the glory of man.

---

[23] Philippians 2:9-11
[24] 1 Corinthians 11:3
[25] Isaiah 9:7
[26] John 5:19
[27] John 16:13-14
[28] John 14:10

# Chapter 9
# A BLESSED MARRIAGE IS A MYSTERY BEING REVEALED

*This is a great mystery, but I speak concerning Christ and the church. Nevertheless let each one of you in particular so love his own wife as himself, and let the wife see that she respects her husband.*[1]

Husband, love your wife!

Wife, respect your husband!

What does that look like? What if they don't deserve it?

> **Only a new creation can truly come into agreement on matters concerning God's order.**

Do you really want what you deserve?

Which would seem closer to the truth—having divine life, but not being in divine order? Or being in divine order, but not having divine life?

One with divine life has only to move into divine order to become fully functional and therefore *fruitful*—the first step of obedience to *The First Commission*.

It is impossible to be in divine order without divine life. Most of what results from such efforts is life-stifling legalism in some sort of stereotypical bondage.

Seeing into the Proverb of the Virtuous Woman[2] as a type of the bride of Christ and a model for all women of all ages ought to

---

[1] Ephesians 5:32-33

dispel forever any stereotypical concepts such as "keeping a woman barefoot in the winter and pregnant in the summer." She was a marvel at managing the home, successful in the marketplace, and a blessing in many areas of society.

There is no stereotype! Only life begets life. We should not give a moment's consideration to what can only produce death. At the same time, to withhold one's self from the maturing process that leads to divine order and fruitful lives would be far less than what God has for us.

Divine order for one couple will undoubtedly look different than divine order for another couple. There are no two fingerprints alike, and there are no two people alike. If there are no two people alike, how can we justify any idea of stereotyping what an ordered and mature marriage might look like?

When God brings two people together to become one, they are often complete opposites. And they complete one another. God knows that they will, in time, blend their lives, motivations, gifts and perspectives into a fruitful marriage and family—male and female, multiplying for God's glory.

Barbara and I were both brought up by parents who believed in God and in fidelity. "Divorce" was not in our dictionary. And neither of us ever experienced any hint of unfaithfulness. Our fathers were good providers; our mothers good homemakers.

We both agreed that the weakness in our respective families was that our fathers were quite passive and our mothers quite aggressive. It was easy to discern our fathers' love for our mothers—not so easy to discern our mothers respect for our fathers.

We were secure in the love of our fathers and still admire them as hard-working and responsible. They "brought home the bacon,"

---

[2] Proverbs 31:10-31

and our moms were very dominant in ruling our households. Our moms laid down their lives for us.

We are within months of celebrating our sixtieth wedding anniversary. Among the keys that we have discovered are differences in the way men and women are mentally and emotionally configured. Physical differences are evident. The mental/emotional differences must also be understood and honored for us to fit together as one in partnership for life.[3] There is much life for me in this Scripture passage:

> *Be good husbands to your wives. Honor them, delight in them. As women they lack some of your advantages. But in the new life of God's grace, you're equals. Treat your wives, then, as equals so your prayers don't run aground.*[4]

Women are created with the need to be loved, and are therefore by nature good at loving. Men are created with the need to be respected and are therefore by nature good at respecting.

So what does God do? He does not order husbands to respect their wives, which would be easy. He does not order wives to love their husbands, which would be easy. No way. Paul wrote:

> *This is a great mystery, but I speak concerning Christ and the church.*
>
> *Nevertheless let each of you in particular love his own wife as himself, and let the wife see that she respects her husband.*[5]

The Holy Spirit gently led us into these truths and equipped our hearts to joyfully respond.

---

[3] Many factors play into individual character structures. We should not stereotype people based upon concepts of masculine and feminine characteristics. Our interactive social natures do not necessarily reflect our hearts.

[4] 1 Peter 3:7 TM

[5] Ephesians 5:32-33

Eroding influences of biblical values have radically changed cultural norms. Kingdom culture and the characteristics necessary for its demonstration in any culture in any time period remain constant. They are the same yesterday, today and forever.

The revelation of this great mystery: The Bridegroom loves us, and we—His bride—are to respect Him.[6] It should be a "no-brainer" to realize that Jesus loves us and we are to respect Him. Add to that the inspired words written by Paul:

> *Let each of you in particular love his own wife as himself, and let the wife see that she respects her husband.*[7]

We should begin to come into agreement that this is far more than a metaphor; this is the strategy of God for revealing a mystery at a very practical human level!

Husbands are to make married life a delightful and secure place of partnership for their wives, at their side, under their arm—exactly as Jesus does His bride.

- *Dwelling with them with understanding*
- *Giving honor to the wife*
- *As to the weaker vessel, and as*
- *Fellow heirs of the grace of life*
- *That your prayers may not be hindered.*[8]

> *Husbands are to love their wives just as Christ also loved the church and gave Himself for her, that He might sanctify and cleanse her with the washing of the word, that He might present her to Himself a glorious church . . .*[9]
> *Woman is (to be) the glory of man.*[10]

---

[6] We do not need to look long or hard to find people who express love for God but fail to respect Him in how they live their lives.
[7] Ephesians 5:32-33
[8] 1 Peter 3:7
[9] Ephesians 5:25-27
[10] 1 Corinthians 11:7

Scripture speaks of *the hidden person of the heart, with the incorruptible beauty of a gentle and quiet spirit, which is very precious in the sight of God.*[11]

I love the tongue-in-cheek yet powerful-in-content poem by Nancy Campbell:

> As for the one who shares my life,
> It was my choice to be his wife!
> And for our jobs, if I could choose,
> I wouldn't want to wear his shoes.
>
> No, I won't sign the lib's petition
> To do away with wife's submission,
> I'd be a fool. to boss my spouse,
> I want a man and not a mouse!
>
> I do not have to prove my might
> For we are equal in God's sight,
> But we're to function differently,
> God made us that way purposely.
>
> He's my provider, what a gem,
> And I'm a helper fit for him.
> To live the role God planned for me
> With joy, makes me completely free![12]

Anyone who has worked with plumbing realizes that male and female fittings are required for them to fit together and properly function. This truth goes much farther and involves much more than "plumbing!"

- God created man in His image.
- Male and female created He them.
- He saw that it was very good.

---

[11] 1 Peter 3:4

[12] www.AboveRubies.org

- He blessed them.

He commissioned them to

- Be fruitful
- Multiply
- Fill the earth and subdue it
- Have dominion

This is *The First Commission*. It provides clarity of identity, purpose and order.

Only a new creation will establish kingdom culture. Only a new creation can truly come into agreement on matters concerning God's order. Those who are limited to their own understanding will continue to seek their own will rather than discover God's liberating will for both male and female counterparts.

God inspired, and Paul wrote these words to a new creation:

> *I want you to know that the head of every man is Christ, the head of woman is man, and the head of Christ is God.*
>
> *For man is not from woman, but woman from man. Nor was man created for the woman, but woman for the man.* [13]
>
> *Wives, submit to your own husband, as to the Lord. For the husband is the head of the wife, as also Christ is head of the church; and He is the Savior of the body.*
>
> *Therefore, just as the church is subject to Christ, so let the wives be to their own husbands in everything.* [14]
> *Wives, submit to your own husbands, as is fitting in the Lord.* [15]

---

[13] 1 Corinthians 11:3; 8-9; Neither is it good for woman to remain alone. She was created from man, for man. So many single women in our neighborhood find their companionship with dogs and cats. That may be the "new normal" but it is not God's normal.
[14] Ephesians 5:22-24

Only those to whom the true nature of spiritual authority has been revealed will be able to rightly process and victoriously walk in what is written regarding kingdom order that manifests kingdom culture.

This is not license for lording it over women. This is a Holy and Divine order that is to release and display nothing less than the fullness of the life of God being lived out in Holy Matrimony. This is a call to a mature mutuality walked in the Spirit. It is a progressive objective, not a static condition.

Even with no cultural implications to deal with, and no history or baggage of their own, Adam and Eve still missed the mark. Both were distracted from divine order.

Submission is an inward attitude; obedience is an outward action. Peter and John humbly submitted to the leaders in Jerusalem when they were set in their midst. But when ordered not to speak at all nor teach in the name of Jesus, they responded:

> *"Whether it is right in the sight of God to listen to you more than to God, you judge. For we cannot but speak the things which we have seen and heard."*[16]

 God knows our hearts. And to Him will we give account. No man has the right to mistreat or abuse his wife in any way. Women should not be intimidated by religious spirits or cultic dogma in this regard.

Bowing down, kneeling and washing the feet of His disciples is an appropriate example of caring for and serving our wives. We should realize that there was a practical service in washing feet in that culture. Surely, the Holy Spirit can reveal to us more practical ways of serving our wives that communicate: "I love you!"

---

[15] Colossians 3:18
[16] Acts 4:19-20

*For we are members of His body, of His flesh and of His bones.*

*"For this reason a man shall leave his father and mother and be joined to his wife, and the two shall become one flesh."[17]*

*"For this reason"* reveals to me that God always intended for this relationship to reveal the joining of Christ and His bride, the church. Oneness in flesh is *"first the natural."* Oneness in spirit is the completion of the plan—the spiritual—so that we may glorify Him in the earth even as *the wife is the glory of her husband.*

*"And the glory which You gave Me I have given them, that they may be one just as We are one; I in them, and You in Me; that they may be made perfect in one, and that the world may know that You have sent Me, and have loved them as You have loved Me."[18]*

A well-loved wife has no trouble respecting her husband.

---

[17] Ephesians 5:30-31; Genesis 2:24
[18] John 17:22-23

# Chapter 10
# FATHERS AND
# THE FAMILY OF GOD

Jesus was being very strategic when teaching His disciples to pray to *"Our Father."*[1]   Later He would assure them, *"He who has seen Me has seen the Father."*[2]

Many still pray, *"Dear Lord . . ."* confessing their servanthood, but not yet relationally impacted as sons. Oh, their belief system may include sonship.   But, their interactions with

> It is much easier to build up a child than it is to repair an adult.

God in reality reveal a very elementary posture in His presence.

"Spiritual Orphans are sin-conscious and carry a spiritual inferiority complex; a sense of unworthiness dominates them. Orphans are ruled by doubt based upon knowing the futility of their flesh.

"Spiritual sons are Father-conscious and carry a spiritual confidence knowing they are affirmed; a sense of acceptance empowers them. Sons are governed by faith based upon knowing Father and the completed work of their elder brother    Jesus!"[3]

The freedom and creative likeness that Adam experienced enabled him to do what no slave could do.   Without the coaching of his Father, he *gave names to all cattle, to the birds of the air, and to every beast of the field.*[4] This was not by the capability of the dust of the earth; this was the enablement of the breath of God in him!

---

[1] Matthew 6:9
[2] John 14:9
[3] Bryon Wiebold
[4] Genesis 2:20

The heart of God's fatherhood was uniquely prophesied by David:

*A father of the fatherless and a judge and protector of the widows is God in His holy habitation.*

*God places the solitary in families and gives the desolate a home in which to dwell; He leads the prisoners out to prosperity; but the rebellious dwell in a parched land.*[5]

Paul revealed two specific traits of our Father that will also be seen in His sons who become fathers: *kindness* and *strict justice.*

*You must try to appreciate both the **kindness** and the **strict justice** of God. Those who fell experienced His justice, while you are experiencing His kindness, and will continue to do so as long as you do not abuse that kindness. Otherwise you too will be cut off from the tree. And as for the fallen branches, unless they are obstinate in their unbelief, they will be grafted in again.*[6]

God, who is perfect everything all the time is the supreme example for fatherhood. He is our model. He is the standard of *perfect love*—the love that *casts out all fear.* Fatherly discipline does not involve torment and does not illicit fear.

*There is no fear in love; but perfect love casts out all fear, because fear involves torment. But he who fears has not been made perfect in love.*[7]

Few grasp the need for balancing these two characteristics, *kindness* and *strict justice.* Among the culture-corrupting failures of the past sixty-five years has been the denigration of fatherhood. There are three major felonies that have served to abort fatherhood from its rightful place within the cultures of nations:

---

[5] Psalm 68:5-6 AMP
[6] Romans 11:22-23 J. B. Phillips NT
[7] 1 John 4:18

- Failing to be *firm*. There are some who walk in the goodness but not the severity required for balanced fathering. They are often guilty of passive abuse, failing to take the lead in training and disciplining their children.[8]

- Failing to be *kind*. There are some who walk in the severity but not the goodness required for balanced fathering. They are often guilty of aggressive abuse—verbal, emotional and/or physical.

- Failing to be present; abandonment. There are many absentee fathers, either gone from the home or ignoring the children as though they were not present in the home.

Those who shepherd God's children also have similar responsibilities, and are often His instruments for *setting in order that which is lacking*[9] in the upbringing of individuals. He pointed out to the church family in Thessalonica how the team "parented" them.

> *We were gentle among you, just as a nursing mother cherishes her own children. So, affectionately longing for you, we were well pleased to impart to you not only the gospel of God, but also our own lives, because you had become dear to us.*
>
> *For you remember, brethren, our labor and toil; for laboring night and day, that we might not be a burden to any of you, we preached to you the gospel of God.*
>
> *You are witnesses, and God also, how devoutly and justly and blamelessly we behaved ourselves among you who believe; as you know how we exhorted, and comforted, and charged every one of you, as a father does his own children, that you should walk worthy of God who calls you into His own kingdom and glory.*[10]

---

[8] Ephesians 6:4; Hebrews 12:11
[9] Titus 1:5

79

Paul does not qualify this passage as being anything less than inspired. These role definitions find their root in the creation story and are consistent with modeling the roles of Christ and His bride, the church.

Many women have been hardened by the need to make up the difference for absentee fathers, being strict and carrying out disciplines which are not natural for them. This leaves children lacking that gentle, cherishing and affectionate mothering, and they are left without the wholeness of either parent. Single moms carry burdens that are not intended for them.

Fathers are to be the primary leaders and disciplinarians.

- Fathers' *exhortation* results in children's *motivation*.
- Fathers' *comfort* results in children's *security*.
- Fathers' *charge* results in awakening children's *destiny*.

Children who are mothered but not fathered are normally gentle and affectionate, often angry at the same time (provoked to wrath by the failure of their fathers). They lack motivation, are insecure, and lack identity, purpose and direction for their lives.

> *If you endure chastening, God deals with you as sons; for what son is there whom a father does not chasten?*
>
> *But if you are without chastening of which all have become partakers, then you are illegitimate and not sons.*
>
> *Furthermore, we have had human fathers who corrected us, and we paid them respect. Shall we not much more readily be in subjection to the Father of spirits and live?*
> *For they indeed for a few days chastened us as seemed best to them, but He for our profit, that we may be partakers of His holiness.*

---

[10] 1 Thessalonians 2:7-12

*Now no chastening seems to be joyful for the present, but painful; nevertheless, afterward it yields the peaceable fruit of righteousness to those who have been trained by it.* [11]

Some baby boomers and those who are younger will want to argue this passage away, consign it to some ancient primitive culture. I plead with you to see the consistent pattern throughout Scripture, and be courageous to embrace God's order. Only if God is out of date is Scripture out of date!

My wife is a loved woman. I am a respected man. Respect comes naturally to men. But we need help with the loving part. "Thank You, Jesus!" Loves comes naturally to women, but they need help with the respect part. "Thank You, Jesus!" How wise of God to require what we cannot provide in our own strength!

Our daughters are baby boomers in years, but kingdom people in life. They respect their husbands who love them, even as we respect Jesus who loves us. Our witness and testimony are intact, and being stewarded by them.

> *This is a great mystery, but I speak concerning Christ and the church. Nevertheless let each one of you in particular love his own wife as himself, and let the wife see that she respects her husband.*
>
> *Children, obey your parents in the Lord, for this is right. "Honor your father and mother," which is the first commandment with promise; "that it may be well with you and you may live long on the earth."*
>
> *And you, fathers, do not provoke your children to wrath, but bring them up in the training and admonition of the Lord.* [12]

---

[11] Hebrews 12:7-11
[12] Ephesians 5:32 – 6:4

It is much easier to build up a child than it is to repair an adult. Choose your words wisely. The answers to life's most important questions are bound up in father/son relationships.

- Who am I? What is my *identity*?
- Where did I come from? What is my *source*?
- Why am I here? What is my *purpose*?
- What can I do? What is my *potential*?
- Where am I going? What is my *destiny*?

The answers to these questions will not be found in a book. While there are some similarities from person to person, each individual needs to discover each specific answer as revelation for himself.

God's original intention is for our natural fathers to be godly men who guide us along toward our maturity in Christ. God also uses godly mentors, those who disciple us toward our maturity in Him.

Of course, it is the discovery of our sonship to Father God that rounds off the hills and fills in the valleys, making *straight paths for our feet.* [13]

> *The Spirit Himself bears witness with our spirit that we are children of God, and if children, then heirs—heirs of God and joint heirs with Christ, if indeed we suffer with Him that we may be glorified together.*
>
> *For I consider that the sufferings of this present time are not worthy to be compared with the glory which shall be revealed in us. For the earnest expectation of the creation eagerly waits for the revealing of the sons of God.* [14]

Do not lightly dismiss the order of God and the need to put Him on display in our everyday lives. We are enabled by the Spirit of Substance. Therefore, what we demonstrate by faith and obedience is compacted with His light and life. And, it is contagious!

---

[13] Hebrews 12:12-13
[14] Romans 8:16-19

Immediately after saying that a bishop *must be blameless*, Paul instructed Timothy that they also must be *the husband of one wife*. It is within the context of family that overseers become qualified:

> *For if a man does not know how to rule his own house, how will he take care of the church of God?*[15]

We should emphasize *take care of the church of God*. Carnal minds do not know how to righteously handle words like *rule*. At best, we are under-shepherds serving the Great Shepherd in caring for His own, including those who are in our families.

Only through personal discipleship will we be prepared for the place that God has prepared for us in His *royal priesthood* and *holy nation*. The priesthood shares His life; the nation His governance.

> *And I heard a loud voice from heaven saying, "Behold, the tabernacle of God is with men, and He will dwell with them, and they shall be His people, God Himself will be with them and be their God.*[16]

Jesus clearly spoke of the priority of the family of God in at least two contexts:

> *"Everyone who has left houses or brothers or sisters or father or mother or wife or children or lands, for My name's sake, shall received a hundredfold, and inherit eternal life."*[17]

> *While He was still talking to the multitudes, behold, His mother and brothers stood outside, seeking to speak with Him. Then one said to Him, "Look, Your mother and Your brothers are standing outside, seeking to speak with You."*

---

[15] 1 Timothy 3:1-7
[16] Revelation 21:2-3
[17] Matthew 19:29

*But He answered and said to the one who told Him, "Who is My mother and who are My brothers?" And He stretched out His hand toward His disciples and said, "Here are My mother and My brothers! For whoever does the will of My Father in heaven is My brother and sister and mother."*[18]

This passage is not justification for alienation from one's nuclear family. The intention of Jesus could not be farther from this. We are to prioritize our spiritual family while at the same time receiving the grace to be fully responsible toward our earthly family—especially honoring our father and our mother.

Jesus fulfilled His final earthly responsibility from the cross by calling upon John to care for His mother:

*Now there stood by the cross of Jesus His mother, and His mother's sister, Mary the wife of Clopas, and Mary Magdalene. When Jesus therefore saw His mother, and the disciple whom He loved standing by, He said to His mother, "Woman, behold your son!" Then He said to the disciple, "Behold your mother!" And from that hour that disciple took her to his own home.*[19]

Historically, it has fallen to the eldest son to guide, provide for and protect family matters in the absence of the father. That responsibility is to be passed through the brothers, in order as each is qualified and capable—even unto the sisters.

In this situation, Jesus connected Mary with John—another practical example of the priority of kingdom family. Jesus knew that John would love His mother as his own.

Paul reminds us of the primary role of fathers:

---

[18] Matthew 12:46-50
[19] John 19:25-27

*After all, though you should have ten thousand teachers (guides to direct you) in Christ, yet you do not have many fathers. For I became your father in Christ Jesus through the glad tidings (the Gospel). So I urge and implore you, be imitators of me.*[20]

*Our [preaching of the] glad tidings (the Gospel) came to you not only in word, but also in [its own inherent] power and in the Holy Spirit and with great conviction and absolute certainty [on our part]. You know what kind of men we proved [ourselves] to be among you for Your good.*

*And you [set yourselves to] become imitators of us and [through us] of the Lord Himself, for you welcomed our message in [spite of] much persecution, with joy [inspired] by the Holy Spirit; so that you [thus] became a pattern to all the believers (those who adhere to, trust in, and rely on Christ Jesus) in Macedonia and Achaia (most of Greece).*[21]

Peter, too, wrote of being examples to the flock:

*Tend (nurture, guard, guide, and fold) the flock of God that is [your responsibility], not by coercion or constraint, but willingly; not dishonorably motivated by the advantages and profits [belonging to the office], but eagerly and cheerfully; not domineering [as arrogant, dictatorial, and overbearing persons] over those in your charge, but being examples (patterns and models of Christian living) to the flock (the congregation).*[22]

Bearing and baring the father heart of God within an antichrist culture is intimidating to some and life-giving to others. Christ shows us the Father and abides in us, enabling fatherhood to be demonstrated through us. Hopefully—prayerfully—our consistent love and pattern will be recognized as *the hope of glory* (Christ in us), to the end that His life and progeny may truly be trans-

---

[20] 1 Corinthians 4:15-16 AMP
[21] 1 Thessalonians 1:5-7 AMP
[22] 1 Peter 5:2-3 AMP

generational, and His glory unceasing. Hopefully, it can be said of us:

"They fulfilled *The First Commission* in their generation!"

# Chapter 11
# MOTHER CHURCH
# AND FATHER GOD

In the forever family, God is our Father and the church is our Mother:

> For it is written that Abraham had two sons: the one by a bondwoman, the other by a freewoman. But he who was of the bondwoman was born according to the flesh, and he of the freewoman through promise, which things are symbolic. For these are the two covenants: the one from Mount Sinai which gives birth to bondage, which is Hagar—for this Hagar is Mount Sinai in Arabia, and corresponds to Jerusalem which now is, and is in bondage with her children—but **the Jerusalem above** is free, which **is the mother of us all.**[1]

> He is her head. She is His helper in shaping our lives for our roles in the kingdom.

> Then I, John, saw the holy city, **New Jerusalem**, coming down out of heaven from God, **prepared as a bride** adorned for her husband.[2]

The Jerusalem that now is refers to an exclusive nationality—then and now, and the Jerusalem above is inclusive of all who are the new creation from every nation in every generation.

> Through Him (Messiah) we both have access by one Spirit to the Father . . . fellow citizens with the saints and members of the household of God.[3]

---

[1] Galatians 4:22-26
[2] Revelation 21:2

(You) *have redeemed us to God by Your blood out of every tribe and tongue and people and nation . . .*[4]

The gentle, affectionate and caring Mother Church[5] is to continually point us to our Father God. That is her role. It is our relationship with Him that *motivates*, makes us *secure*, and *envisions* us for our destined places in His body and our roles in His kingdom. When we hear God say: *"This is My beloved Son, in whom I am well-pleased,"*[6] we are changed forever!

He is her head. She is His helper in shaping our lives for our roles in the kingdom. We are not created for the church. We are created for Father's eternal family. Hidden down inside each individual is something that we call "potential." It is actually more than our potential; it's our spiritual DNA, who we really are in Christ.

> *Beloved, now we are children of God; and it has not yet been revealed what we shall be, but we know that when He is revealed, we shall be like Him, for we shall see Him as He is.*[7]

At Father God's direction, Mother Church collectively nurtures us, helping us to recognize and realize who our Father is and that we are created in His image. She reminds us regularly that our Father never goes AWOL, He *never leaves nor forsakes* us,[8] He is *with us always*.[9]

I learned to clearly establish Barbara's authority in the home and to undergird her. I would say to the children when preparing to leave, "Your mother is in charge, and I will ask her for a report when I

---

[3] Ephesians 2:18-19
[4] Revelation 5:9
[5] The term "Mother Church" sometimes refers to the founding assembly of a group of assemblies. *"The Jerusalem above"* is the eternal church, "the mother of us all."
[6] Matthew 3:17
[7] 1 John 3:2
[8] Matthew 28:20
[9] Hebrews 13:5

return." (You must receive this within the context of a good and proactive relationship with our children to accurately hear what my heart intends to communicate.)

Have you ever noticed that children respond differently to mothers and fathers? Mama can plead, order, command several times without getting a response. Dad says it once in a normal voice and the kids jump. They love Mama; the respect Dad.

It is the same in the family of God. The church can say it over and over without getting a response. But, when Father God speaks, we listen. And we jump to obey!

"I hate you!" is not an uncommon phrase coming from children upset because they are not getting their way. Crushing to good moms, Dad is most likely to say. "That's fine. You'll get over it. And you will respect and obey me!" God can handle our emoting and rejecting.

God has established the authority of the church, and He undergirds it. (Remember Ananias and Sapphira?) Jesus spent the entire night with Him prior to calling the twelve disciples who would become the apostles of the Lamb. He is in the midst of apostles appointing elders in every city. He oversees the discipling of each individual.

Church fathers—elders—oversee the process, prayerfully and carefully guiding those whose hands-on responsibilities are molding us in cooperation with the Holy Spirit.

Equipping ministry gifts are identified in Scripture as *apostles, prophets, evangelists, and shepherds and teachers.*[10] The several members of Mother Church are also necessary, because who we are and what we do will be incomplete as long as we are functioning only as individuals.

Make no mistake. Father has a future in mind for each one of us, and church leaders are to equip us for His purpose,[11]

---

[10] Ephesians 4:11

*. . . till we all come to the unity of the faith and of the knowledge of the Son of God, to a perfect man, to the measure of the stature of the fullness of Christ . . . from whom the whole body, joined and knit together by what every joint supplies, according to the effective working by which every part does its share, causes growth of the body for the edifying of itself in love.*[12]

Following are some general insights into these five significant questions regarding our lives:

- **Who am I? What is my *identity*?** I am a son of God, not simply by adoption, but I also have His genes, His DNA, through spiritual birth.

- **Where did I come from? What is my *source*?** I am born from above. Where am I from? I am from heaven, and all of the resources of heaven are available as I walk in the Spirit.

- **Why am I here? What is my *purpose*?** I am to glorify (show forth) the life of God by conforming to His image and being equipped for the works that He prepared beforehand for me to do.

- **What can I do? What is my *potential*?** I can do all things through Christ who strengthens me. I can become everything He wants me to be; and do everything He wants me to do.

- **Where am I going? What is my *destiny*?** I am destined for His eternal kingdom as part of His forever family.

Whatever it takes to get me there He will provide as I rest in obedience to Him.

---

[11] Ephesians 2:10
[12] Ephesians 4:13-16

Jesus underscored the value of having the answers to the above life's questions by His own testimony:

> *Jesus once again addressed [the Pharisees]: "I am the world's Light. No one who follows Me stumbles around in the darkness. I provide plenty of light to live in."*
>
> *The Pharisees objected, "All we have is your word on this. We need more than this to go on."*
>
> *Jesus replied, "You're right that you only have My word. But you can depend on it being true. **I know where I've come from and where I go next. You don't know where I'm from or where I'm headed.** You decide according to what you can see and touch. I don't make judgments like that. But even if I did, My judgment would be true because I wouldn't make it out of the narrowness of my experience but in the largeness of the One who sent Me, the Father. That fulfills the conditions set down in God's Law: that you can count on the testimony of two witnesses. And that is what you have: You have My word and you have the word of the Father who sent Me."*
>
> *They said, "Where is this so-called Father of yours?"*
>
> *Jesus said, "You're looking right at Me and you don't see Me. How do you expect to see the Father? If you knew Me, you would at the same time know the Father."*[13]

To exude such confidence in the face of oppressors requires us to have specific and very personally applicable answers. These normally come to us within the context of being fathered.

Father God instructed Jeremiah to *"Arise and go down to the potter's house, and there I will cause you to hear My words."*[14]

---

[13] John 8:12-19 TM
[14] Jeremiah 18:1-4

This was one of those special learning times when God allowed Jeremiah insights from a natural process that could be a metaphor. While the Scripture does not specifically say this, let me tell you one thing that this metaphor has shown me:

Potters use both hands when shaping a vessel—one hand on the inside, and one hand on the outside. Otherwise, we cannot keep the vessel on the wheel. It is vital, essential, for both hands to work together in coordination to get it right with the potter's vision.

The church, *which is the mother of us all,* represented at any given moment or season by a particular group or individual,[15] is God's *hand on the outside,* and the Holy Spirit is *the Hand on the inside.* The Holy Spirit is also still the Hand on the inside of the one(s) doing the discipling and equipping, making it possible for both to work in complete conjunction and coordination with one another.

Failure to carefully and prayerfully bring adjustments only as led by the Spirit can do much damage. Our independent actions can push the clay completely off the wheel! Fortunately, Father God and Mother Church are one in the Spirit, even as husbands and wives become one flesh.

Mother Church is to reflect Father God's glory, and is exhorted:

> *Do not let your adornment be merely outward—arranging the hair, wearing gold, or putting on fine apparel[16]—rather let it be the hidden person of the heart, with the incorruptible beauty of a gentle and quiet spirit, which is very precious in the sight of God.*

---

[15] It is common and normal for a particular person to be discipling a novice. Galatians 4:1-2 illustrates this principle from the prevailing culture of that time: *Now I say that the heir, as long as he is a child, does not differ at all from a slave, though he is master of all, but is under guardians and stewards until the time appointed by the father.*

[16] Consider this as a metaphor for how the church in our city is to represent herself.

*For in this manner, in former times, the holy women who trusted in God also adorned themselves, being submissive to their own husbands, as Sarah obeyed Abraham, calling him lord, whose daughters you are if you do good and are not afraid with any terror.*[17]

This is quite a challenge for today's churches. Yet, how can we so easily dismiss such a clear and holy design? Wise master builders (spiritual architects) are, with the Holy Spirit, to mold local and regional expressions of the bride of Christ that make Him desirable,[18] but not compromised by Babylonian taste buds.[19]

Once again we are reminded of a great mystery:

*This mystery is very great, but I speak concerning [the relation of] Christ and the church.*

*However, let each man of you [without exception] love his wife as [being in a sense] his very own self; and let the wife see that she respects and reverence her husband [that she notices him, regards him, honors him, prefers him, venerates, and esteems him; and that she defers to him, praises him, and loves and admires him exceedingly].*[20]

Moving on into maturity and wholeness, people should begin to grasp how Jesus loves by observing how husbands love their lives. And they should also be impressed on how they are to respond to Jesus by watching how wives respect their husbands.

They should begin to see into the great mystery as they have it modeled before their eyes.

It becomes increasingly obvious that fulfilling *The First Commission* is the shared responsibility of the bride of Christ, the mother of us all. This is a comprehensive assignment that can only

---

[17] 1 Peter 3:3-6
[18] Your desire shall be for your husband – Genesis 3:16
[19] The lust of the flesh, the lust of the eyes, and the pride of life – 1 John 2:16
[20] Ephesians 5:32-33; [I Peter 3:2] AMP

be carried out by a new creation living life—the life of Christ—in the Spirit.

# Chapter 12
# CONVERTING CHURCH MEMBERS TO DISCIPLES

Dying to ourselves is an absolute requirement for living in the Spirit. Living in the Spirit is an absolute requirement for fulfilling the First Commission.

Deitrich Bonhoeffer said, "The call to Christ is a call to come and die." I would add: ". . . daily, sometimes hourly." The life of a disciple is constantly being born out of death.

> "One-anothering" became a high priority.

> . . . always carrying about in the body the dying of the Lord Jesus, that the life of Jesus also may be manifest in our body. For we who live are always delivered to death for Jesus's sake, that the life of Jesus also may be manifested in our mortal flesh. So then death is working in us, but life in you.[1]

If I am discipling you, and I fail to die to myself so that Jesus may be seen, you will end up looking like me instead of Him. Perish the thought!

Backing up just a few verses, we find this explanation:

> We have this treasure in earthen vessels, that the excellence of the power may be of God and not us.[2]

There is no legitimate way to call others to discipleship than for us to exemplify and model life as disciples. Disciples make disciples

---

[1] 2 Corinthians 4:10-12
[2] 2 Corinthians 4:7

after kind. Jesus worked into His disciples what His Father had worked into Him. Great sons are the workmanship of great fathers who themselves eventually become great fathers reproducing great sons.

- *He who believes in Me, the works that I do he will do also; and greater works than these he will do, because I go to My Father.*[3]

- *For we are His workmanship, created in Christ Jesus for good works, which God prepared beforehand that we should walk in them.*[4]

Those whom God joins to us in the Spirit are attracted to the Christ in us and have the desire to follow our example.

> *For our gospel did not come to you in word only, but in power, and in the Holy Spirit and in much assurance, as you know what kind of men we were among you for your sake.*

> *And **you became followers of us and of the Lord**, having received the word in much affliction, with joy of the Holy Spirit, so that **you became examples to all** in Macedonia and Achaia who believe.*[5]

We don't get very far along in reading the first chapter of Genesis before realizing that everything reproduces after kind!

I accepted an invitation to speak at a traditional Christian Church on Easter, 1973. As I stood at the door shaking hands with people as they were leaving, the common chorus was, "I hope that you will be our minister!"—the farthest thing from my mind!

As I realized the commonality, I also noticed a group of men in the front of the auditorium in a serious, impromptu meeting. As the

---

[3] John 14:12
[4] Ephesians 2:10
[5] 1 Thessalonians 1:5-7

last people were leaving they came and asked if I would be interested in moving there and serving as minister.

We adjourned to the church office, and I was totally candid with them, specifically spelling out beliefs that I held that I knew were contrary to their historical positions. Somehow, God quickly moved us past all of those stones of stumbling, and we soon found ourselves living in their parsonage and serving as minister.

There were several young families who were immediately drawn to our young family, and the process of discipleship seemed to be underway by a sovereign move of God. How we loved these families! How they loved us! They quickly moved from being traditional church members to disciples of Christ under our care. We added new converts who understood the nature of commitment required to be a disciple before making their commitment.

What we didn't realize at the time was that (a) the congregation voted annually whether or not to retain the minister, and he needed a two-third vote to stay. And, (b) one family controlled the church. The patriarch and his two middle-aged sons were three of the five elders. (Go figure!)

The building was packed out on voting day with grandchildren of the patriarch and their families. We met dozens of people we had not seen in the entire year of our tenure. The vote was quickly counted, and sixty-five percent of the people wanted us to stay. The patriarch and his family had a voting block of thirty-five percent.

Without our planning or participation, our Father had scheduled our deliverance from that situation before we ever entered into it. Not only were we delivered, but all of those who had become disciples were also set free.

During that year, we had befriended the minister and several others from a small Church of Christ just a few blocks away. The Holy Spirit was transforming many in that membership at the same time.

We immediately merged the two groups of disciples. The other minister was a gifted teacher, but willing to allow me to lead what was now an emerging fellowship of dozens of young families.

Wednesday evenings found us together singing and dancing and clapping in harmonious unison. What was being bred and born in praise and worship would eventually expand to more and more areas of life. Life was our target; family worshiping together was our initial strategy.

Blankets and sleeping bags at the feet of parents accommodated the little ones who would become exceedingly bored by the teaching, dialogue and ministry that followed the singing. Children who were old enough were taught to sit quietly, even take notes and participate in any dialogue.

It is amazing what can come out of the mouths of babes! Truly, *a little child shall lead them!*[6] Jesus made it very clear: *"Of such is the kingdom of God."*[7]

We remember one little four-year-old boy who had a bonafide gift of healing. Whenever the elders were called upon to pray, anointing with oil, Danny was there in the midst of them, laying hands upon the one needing healing. Inevitably, if Danny prayed, someone was healed!

Sunday school was family oriented with each set of parents taking their turns in the nursery—men included. Rather than "canned" curriculum we developed subjects practical for these parents of young children—all about family—learning from one another about family devotions and parental disciplines, etc.

Fathers were challenged and charged with the responsibility of bringing their children up in the training and admonition of the Lord, rather than provoking them to wrath by failure to do so. Parents were coached on how to present a united and loving front

---

[6] Isaiah 11:6
[7] Luke 18:16

before their children, resolving their differences behind closed doors.

Children prospered under the application of the loving rod of correction. We actually had little children come and say, "Daddy, I need the rod!" Daddy would take them to a private place, inquire why, and—after discussion—take the appropriate action. Whatever the action, the final phase was holding the child in his arms and expressing love, acceptance and forgiveness. The consciences of the children became pure because of the freedom to "dump" their "sin" and believe that they were forgiven. They became confident in their faith at very young ages.

We lived life together in community.[8] We added to the security level for all of the children and the parents as we shared life, love, and oversight together—always honoring and respecting the family identities within.

The felt need for Sunday school disappeared over time. "One-anothering" became a high priority. Leadership was multiplying and outreaches thriving.

There was an overwhelming "Shalom" both in our assembling and in the individual homes—evidence of the increasing government of God in us as individuals, families and as an expression of the church.

> *Of the increase of His government and peace there will be no end.*[9]

Located in an area of vineyards, one-third of the congregation was Mexican. We had wonderful potluck dinners! One of our recent converts was a Mexican man who owned and operated a bar. Immediately upon his conversion he put the bar on the market. But, God didn't let it sell for three years. That bar became a primary evangelistic center!

---

[8] Not all together in a commune, but rather each family unit in its own home with open hearts, doors and availability 24/7/365.

[9] Isaiah 9:7

My first missionary journey beyond the borders of the United States was to Mexico with him—a life-changing time that prepared my heart for many journeys into dozens of nations in the years to follow.

Admittedly, we were working with a small number of people. That's how discipleship works. Jesus chose twelve with whom to live life in order to prepare them for leadership. We know that He also sent out another seventy on at least one occasion. And, we also know there were about one hundred twenty in the upper room on Pentecost.

They were in one accord—waiting—unwilling to make a move unless and until the Holy Spirit moved them. We learned from these biblical patterns to not live by principles, but to live His life in the Spirit. Once again, Scripture leaves us without the convenience of stereotyping! Life begets life.

Some people left to search out a more comfortable religious environment. We blessed them in their going. We were *missional*, not *situational*. It is better to live in one accord with a smaller number of disciples than to compromise for numbers.

There was kingdom fruit and multiplication on many levels that included multinational and multigenerational ministry life. ***The First Commission*** was at the forefront of our lives.

# Chapter 13
# DARE TO BEGIN AT THE BEGINNING

Many have begun developing their theological understanding and world view somewhere after the beginning. Some are steeped in denominational history and dogma. Others build from the Reformation forward. Still others begin at Azusa Street, or the Latter Rain.

Somehow, God spared me of all the little "boxes" that "contain" and severely handicap so many. Someone once remarked that I drank from many streams without falling into any of them! At the same time, I always respect the prevailing authority without judging his/her legitimacy, thus bringing judgment on myself by so doing.[1]

> **What we thought were contradictions simply needed the greater illumination of the newer version!**

I began reading in Genesis Chapter 1, and have always believed that God created me—male, and made for me a helper—Barbara—female, both in His image, then blessed us, and instructed us *to be fruitful and multiply; fill the earth and subdue it; have dominion over . . . every living thing that moves on the earth.*

Our first tool for dominion business was a flyswatter. It wasn't long until dominion moved to a new level—potty-training our children. If we cannot find application for God's will in the most simple and practical matters, we surely have no business floating around in a mystical universe with no absolutes.

---

[1] Romans 12:1-2

We had four daughters who gave us twelve grandchildren who, so far, have given us sixteen great-grandchildren. We are impressed with modern technology, none greater than disposable diapers!

During those early years I heard myself telling others things that I just knew were true, but had never heard or read them before. They were as new to me as to the ones with whom I was talking. No problem. I knew that God had written these things on my heart and was not surprised when I would find these truths in Scripture—a week, a month, or even years later. (Why do so many make Christianity so difficult and complicated?)

The New Covenant must be a new covenant that replaces the old covenant. A change of covenants does not mean that God has changed His mind. Simple logic comes in really handy. How could there be two covenants with contradictions simultaneously in effect? But, wait. Given enough time we realize that what we thought were contradictions simply needed the greater illumination of the newer version!

Perhaps you can envision with me circling an inverted mountain of truth beginning at the top. Our first time around we think we've got it. But, every time we circle the inverted mountain we go deeper and find deeper truth. Bottom line, no matter how old we are, or how many times we have circled the inverted mountain, and no matter how deep we have gone into certain truths, we had better stick with the priority of love.

> *Love will cover a multitude of sins.*[2]

> *Love never fails.*

> *But whether there are prophecies, they will fail; whether there are tongues, they will cease; whether there is knowledge, it will vanish away.*

> *For we know in part and we prophesy in part.*

---

[2] 1 Peter 4:8

*But when that which is perfect has come, then that which is in part will be done away.*

*When I was a child, I spoke as a child, I understood as a child, I thought as a child; but when I became a man, I put away childish things.*

*For now we see in a mirror, dimly, but then face to face. Now I know in part, but then I shall know just as I also am known.*

*And now abide faith, hope, love, these three; but*

*The greatest is love.*[3]

Now, fifty years later, I still remain free of the mind-boggling confusion that keeps so many adrift without a sure foundation. My foundation is a Person who has proven Himself time and again— not a book, not a doctrine—a person. I don't need to go anywhere, don't need special times, places or people. At the same time, I am free to love, embrace and enjoy His family—my fellow family members—in any venue.

Wherever I go, He is! He never leaves me. In simplistic terms this is the apostolic foundation that is to be laid by God's master builders.

Jesus Himself prophesied what would take place and transform His disciples at Pentecost:

*"I will not leave you orphans; I will come to you. A little while longer and the world will see Me no more, but you will see Me. Because I live, you will live also. At that day you will know that I am in My Father, and you in Me, and I in you."*[4]

---

[3] 1 Corinthians 13:8-13
[4] John 14:18-20

Paul questioned the people in Corinth: *Do you not know yourselves, that Jesus Christ is in you? If you don't, you are disqualified.*[5] You have failed the litmus test[6] confirming whose are His.

An affirmative response to this question—"Yes, Jesus Christ is in me!"—brings together in one: *Jews and Greeks, slaves and free, male and female.*[7]

> *For through Him we both (all who know that Christ is in us) have access by one Spirit to the Father. Now, therefore, you are no longer strangers and foreigners, but fellow citizens with the saints and members of the household of God, having been built on the foundation of the apostles and prophets, Jesus Christ Himself being the chief cornerstone, in whom the whole building, being fitted together, grows into a holy temple of the Lord, in whom you also are being built together for a dwelling place of God in the Spirit.*[8]

Paul went on:

> *By revelation He made known to me the mystery (as I have briefly written already, by which, when you read, you may understand my knowledge in the mystery of Christ), which in other ages was not made known to the sons of men, as it has now been revealed by the Spirit to His holy apostles and prophets; that the Gentiles should be fellow heirs, of the same body, and partakers of His promise in Christ through the gospel.*[9]

Once again, Paul clarifies that he is the benefactor of being graced to preach *the unsearchable riches of Christ, and to make all see what is the fellowship of the mystery . . . to the intent that the*

---

[5] 2 Corinthians 13:5
[6] "Litmus" is a test that uses a single indicator to prompt a decision.
[7] Galatians 3:26-29
[8] Ephesians 2:18-22
[9] Ephesians 3:3-6

*manifold wisdom of God might be made known by the church to the principalities and powers in the heavenly places.*[10]

We can gain a vital insight into the higher ways of God by Paul's words above. He made it clear that his knowledge of the mystery came by revelation, revealed by the Spirit, and that he was graced to preach the unsearchable riches of Christ.

Things about Christ that are established historical facts are *searchable*. However, the mystery of Christ Himself is *unsearchable* and comes only by the revelation of the Spirit— commonly revealed to His holy apostles and prophets. It is **not the history *about*** Jesus Christ that is foundational to the church; it **is the mystery *of* Jesus Christ** that is the revelation of the foundation. Paul wrote to the Corinthians,

> *According to the grace of God which was given to me, as a wise master builder I have laid the foundation, and another builds on it. But let each one take heed how he builds on it.*
>
> *For no other foundation can anyone lay than that which is laid, which is Jesus Christ.*[11]

It is out of that Holy Spirit-inspired confidence that we can press forward in pursuit of our family, those with whom we can come into agreement regarding Him (not to be confused with needing to agree on every jot and tittle). If we each play our part according to the score at the downbeat and the timing of the Holy Director, we will *make beautiful music together.*

> *"Truly I tell you, whatever you forbid and declare to be improper and unlawful on earth must be what is already forbidden in heaven, and whatever you permit and declare proper and lawful on earth must be what is already permitted in heaven."*

---

[10] Ephesians 3:8-13
[11] 1 Corinthians 3:10-11

(This is the simple explanation of how the kingdom operates—with two in agreement, Father God and Mother Church. It is our agreement first with God and then with one another that calls heaven down to earth.)

> *"Again I tell you, if two of you on earth agree (harmonize together, make a symphony together) about whatever [anything and everything] they may ask, it will come to pass and be done for them by My Father in heaven.*
>
> *"For wherever two or three are gathered (drawn together as My followers) in (into) My name, there I AM in the midst of them."*[12]

We have complicated and compromised "church," primarily by focusing upon it. Most attendees do not participate in The Great Commission, and have never heard of The First Commission (except possibly in a "Bible story"). They *go to* church rather than *being* the church.

Role confusion translates into authority confusion. It is commonplace in today's religious culture for some to believe that Mother Church and her constituents have equal authority with Father God! When *Head* and *helper* are mutually independent, both purpose and the substance of purpose are lost in the confusion.

In so many circles, people offer a brief token prayer to affirm God and supposedly request His guidance and blessing, and then go on to promoting the leader's vision (more likely their own) for personal success.

None of these blasphemies would have any substance if they were not given substance by man. God's First Commission is clear:

1. Be fruitful
2. Multiply

---

[12] Matthew 18:18-20 AMP

3. Fill the earth
4. Subdue it
5. Reign

What cannot you understand about that? Is that not simple enough for a child to grasp?

We would not have been able to take the first step of obedience to **The First Commission** had we not been created *male and female*.

> In [the plan of] the Lord and from His point of view woman is not apart from and independent of man, nor is man aloof from and independent of woman; for as woman was made from man, even so man is also born of woman; and all [whether male or female go forth] from God [as their Author].[13]

A radical commitment to obedient discipleship can still propel a people into places of faith that will release *grace according to the measure of Christ's gift.*[14]

If I were cynical, I would not have given myself to this writing. I am hopeful, and praying against spirits of lawlessness and independence—praying for the merging of minds and lives into the design and order of God.

Those who are His have already received the *anointing.* It is *trust and obedience* that is needed.

---

[13] 1 Corinthians 11:11-12 AMP
[14] Ephesians 4:7

# Chapter 14
# POTPOURRI WITH SIMPLEXITY

This is the golden anniversary of my birth into a new creation—fifty years of incredibly abundant living[1] that has taken us through a host of growing experiences.

The thought came to me, "How would I describe my journey in a word?" As I meditated on the question, the word came to me.

*Simplexity!*

*Simplexity* is a combination of *simplicity* and *complexity,* which—for me—explains the journey of these past fifty years.

> Increasing insights and revelation enlarge Him, not us. The moment we believe that we are being enlarged in our own eyes, *pride* has come.

*Potpourri* is a combination of incongruous things, thoughts, experiences, etc. that has contributed to my life of *simplexity.*

It is a huge challenge, especially for those who are called to be servant-leaders, to "keep it simple" when the very demands of your role requires searching into complexity (not to mention the demands of the human ego). Realizing that those who teach *receive a stricter judgment*[2] adds even more weightiness to the matter. Seemingly, there is a contradiction between simplicity and complexity:

---

[1] We have found that *prosperity* is *having what you need when you need it.* That is *abundant living* for those who lay up our treasures in heaven's realm.

[2] James 3:1

*But I fear, lest somehow, as the serpent deceived Eve by his craftiness, so your minds may be corrupted from the simplicity that is in Christ.*[3]

*Be diligent to present yourself approved of God, a worker who does not need to be ashamed, rightly dividing the word of truth.*[4]

Don't those two verses seem to contradict one another? Frankly, I spent many years amazing myself with all of the complexities that can go along with expanding understanding of God and His plan and purpose for our lives. I admit that there have been seasons when I lost touch with *the simplicity that is in Christ*—and I don't recommend it.

Oswald Chambers points out that: "To be 'in the will of God' is not a matter of intellectual discernment, but a state of heart."

Intellectually comprehendible concepts and conclusions can be mind corrupters, faith stealers. When complexities begin to compound, we must remember that we are continually received into the kingdom as little children awed by *the simplicity that is in Christ*. Increasing insights and revelation enlarge Him, not us. The moment we realize that we are being enlarged in our own eyes, *pride* has come. Can a *fall* be far away?

*Pride goes before destruction, and a haughty spirit before a fall. Better to be a humble spirit with the lowly, than to divide the spoil with the proud.*[5]

"The Gospel is not that the good are in & the bad are out; it's that the humble are in & the proud are out."[6]

---

[3] 2 Corinthians 11:3
[4] 2 Timothy 2:15
[5] Proverbs 16:18-19
[6] Tim Keller

Get this, and never allow knowledge to puff you up again! Standing in a safe place within *the simplicity that is in Christ*, we can accommodate that which enlarges Jesus in our sight and our understanding, resulting in humility—not arrogance.

It is recorded in Scripture that, immediately following Pentecost when the believers' only credential was that the were filled with the Holy Spirit:

> *So continuing daily with one accord in the temple, and breaking bread from house to house, they ate their food with gladness and simplicity of heart.*[7]

I was brought to tears while watching the last few minutes of a movie filmed by the Billy Graham Evangelistic Association last evening. I sensed the powerful effect that God has had upon multitudes through this man. Billy Graham was greatly gifted in communicating *the simplicity that is in Christ.*

Next we watched "Precious Memories, how they linger . . ."— produced by Bill Gaither. This week featured the Happy Goodmans. All of these people are my peers and represent a culture that is foreign to younger people

Bill and Gloria Gaither, Howard and Vestal Goodman, and so many others have always communicated a testimony of *the simplicity that is in Christ.* Vestal sang this:

> From the dust of the earth my God created man –
> His breath made man a living soul:
> And God so loved the world He gave His only Son,
> And that is why I love Him so!
>
> My hands were made to help my neighbor,
> My eyes were made to read God's word.
> My feet were made to walk in His footsteps,
> My body is the temple of the Lord.

---

[7] Acts 2:46

I was made in His likeness, created in His image,
For I was born to serve the Lord.
I will not deny Him, I will always walk beside Him,
For I was born to serve the Lord.[8]

Jesus is the equalizer. Regardless of how severe our intellectual limitations, the fullness of Christ dwells in each of us. We can never gain more of Him. We have all of Him in His fullness! We can only grow to know more of the One who abides inside of us. My mind has been changed several times, but:

*Jesus Christ is the same yesterday, today, and forever.*[9]

Just this afternoon I received an email causing me concern about the doctrinal position of a brother whom I love very much. The moment that I turned to God with the issue, He reminded me of His capacity to look beyond what is going on in our heads, and to see what's going on in our hearts! Jesus is the answer to extreme cerebralitis, even the strains induced by religious spirits.

I am blessed with spiritual children scattered to many nations. They do not agree with me in every intellectual detail. That is wonderful. They are fully His and that is the basis for our ongoing fellowship in Him. We agree in those things that pertain to godly character and integrity. They are "after kind" which is fruit of their discipleship. Intellectual liberty is essential. Otherwise we end up with clones created with cookie cutters.

We may not always be able to see into the hearts of others. But He is eager to provide grace for us so that we might trust Him, bear witness with our brothers, and enjoy our fellowship with one another without getting bent out of shape by *every wind of doctrine*[10] that sometimes carries our loved ones (and us) to places of error and excess.

---

[8] Words and Music by Janet Trout
[9] Hebrews 13:8
[10] Ephesians 4:14

I know numerous people—some of my grandchildren for example—who profoundly love their various churches and are abounding in life. So, when I address matters such as those written in this book, I have no intention or desire to belittle another who may not see it the way I do. Lots of good things are going on, and many are being blessed and are growing *in the grace and knowledge of our Lord and Savior Jesus Christ. To Him be the glory both now and forever.*[11]

> *Knowledge makes arrogant, but love edifies.*

Bryan Corbin says: "Arrogance is not the byproduct of overconfidence, it is the facade we build around our deepest insecurities."

> *If anyone supposes that he knows anything, he has not yet known as he ought to know; but if anyone loves God, he is known by Him.*[12]

A comprehensive definition of love is summarized by putting knowledge into perspective:

> *For now we see in a mirror, dimly, but then face to face.*

> *Now I know in part, but then I shall know just as I am known.*

> *And now abide faith, hope, love, these three; but the greatest of these is love.*[13]

> *Love covers a multitude of sins.*[14]

> Love never fails.[15]

---

[11] 2 Peter 3:18
[12] 1 Corinthians 8:1-3
[13] 1 Corinthians 13:12-13
[14] 1 Peter 4:8
[15] 1 Corinthians 13:8a

It will require an unusual measure of grace for us to embrace *The First Commission* in faith. Filling the earth will come one day and one mile at a time. It will begin by realizing our oneness in Christ. This is not something that we do; it's something we believe and receive. Jesus did it. It's a done deal!

It won't happen trying to sort out particular doctrines. It will happen as we recognize and adapt to a proper litmus test for authentic Christianity:

> *Examine yourselves as to whether you are in the faith. Test yourselves. Do you not know yourselves, that Jesus Christ is in you?—unless indeed you are disqualified.*[16]

> *The Spirit Himself bears witness with our spirit that we are children of God.*[17]

All who are in Christ, all in whom Christ abides, are included in the new creation, His present-day body on the earth. We have eternity to get our heads around "stuff." In the meantime, we can abide in the vine and bring forth much fruit. That translates into multiplication.

Discipling the nations is God's strategy for instituting and perpetrating His kingdom on earth as it is in heaven. Multiplication will eventually fill the earth with His glory.

> *Let this mind be in you which was also in Christ Jesus, who, being in the form of God did not consider it robbery to be equal with God, but made Himself of no reputation, taking the form of a bondservant, and coming in the likeness of men. And being found in appearance as a man, He humbled Himself and became obedient to the point of death, even the death of the cross.*

---

[16] 2 Corinthians 13:5

[17]

*Therefore God also has highly exalted Him and given Him the name which is above every name, that at the name of Jesus every knee should bow, of those in heaven, and of those on earth, and of those under the earth, and that every tongue should confess that Jesus Christ is Lord, to the glory of God the Father.*[18]

Jesus provides His portion for our obedience to *The First Commission.* He has taken up permanent residence within His disciples to guide us in discipling nations.

God is bringing many sons to glory—Jesus being the first of many—that all the earth be filled with His glory.

I know that I am not alone in my *simplexity.*

---

[18] Philippians 2:5-11

Made in United States
North Haven, CT
24 May 2024